AF539778

THINK LIKE A YOGI

Ancient Indian Secrets for Long, Happy & Purposeful Life

THINK LIKE A YOGI

Ancient Indian Secrets for Long, Happy & Purposeful Life

ROHIT MEHRA, IRS

PRABHAT PRAKASHAN

Published by
PRABHAT PRAKASHAN PVT. LTD.
4/19 Asaf Ali Road,
New Delhi-110002 (INDIA)
e-mail: prabhatbooks@gmail.com

ISBN 978-93-5562-250-1
THINK LIKE A YOGI
by *Rohit Mehra, IRS*

Edition
2025

Price
₹ 700 (Rupees Seven Hundred Only)

Printed at
Japan Art, Delhi

Dedicated to all those who aspire to be their best selves, seeking a life of simplicity, happiness, and purpose. In deep reverence, I acknowledge my profound indebtedness to the ancient Indian culture, a timeless heritage that transcends boundaries and resonates with the essence of humanity.

Author's Note

Are you content with your life at this moment? If not, do you desire a change? Have you pondered why you long for change? Think, think. Hmm! Let's think about it.

Everyone desires change. The yearning for change is universal. You seek change because you are unhappy with your current state of your life, believing that changing it will bring you happiness. It pre-supposes a feeling of unhappiness, dissatisfaction and frustration with how things currently in life are.

You might want a change in your daily routine, health, family relationships, finances, career, free time, and so on.

Essentially, people seek change primarily because they are unhappy. The driving force of human life is happiness, influencing every action and decision made on this planet. As humans, we aspire ongoing happiness—today, tomorrow, and forever. This aspiration goes beyond momentary happiness; it extends to a desire for continuous joy in all moments of life.

Indeed, the pursuit is for maximum happiness. When faced with choices between two happy situations, the desire is to choose the one that brings more happiness. For instance, if you enjoy both juice and cold coffee, you'll likely choose cold coffee if that brings you greater happiness.

This quest for more happiness is innate in all humans, irrespective of age, location, or circumstances. For instance, my son Dhruv, in the 11th standard, prefers playing games over reading a book because it brings him more happiness. Despite the logical and rational suggestion that he should prioritize studying at this crucial stage in life, the pursuit of happiness often takes precedence.

Absolutely, the pursuit of happiness influences every aspect of our lives. From small decisions like what to eat or how to dress, to significant choices such as selecting a career, our thoughts, actions, and efforts are guided by the desire for happiness. It serves as a constant measure influencing our decisions both big and small. This pursuit of happiness decides the very purpose of human life. Purpose is the journey while happiness is the destination.

Happiness can be achieved in two ways: by avoiding non-desirable things and circumstances or by pursuing desirable things. The history of mankind is the history of efforts bringing changes in the life and circumstances of the existing states of human beings. Indeed, the continuous pursuit of happiness has driven mankind to create a plethora of comforts, luxuries, and wonders.

This includes advancements in wealth, scientific inventions, and medical facilities, all aimed at enhancing the well-being and quality of life for individuals and societies. Exactly, many of the inventions of modern science are geared towards providing comforts and luxuries with the ultimate goal of reducing human suffering and discomfort.

They are aimed at comforting us. To reduce the tiring pain of walking, we invented cycles, bikes, cars, bullet trains, aero planes, etc,. Similarly, we have constructed big skyscrapers, malls, air-conditioners, mobiles and host of other gadgets just to make our life happy and comfortable.

Many people tend to equate happiness with comfort, yet the true purpose of life is happiness. This pursuit of understanding happiness is a fundamental aspect of the human experience. But the problem is that most people do not know what exactly is happiness, where and how to find this happiness and which things and thoughts give them true happiness?

Modern ethos of self-development often suggests that happiness can be achieved through outer success. Success, however, varies from person to person—some aspire to be doctors, others engineers, musicians, and so forth. Almost every one of us wants to be rich. If you ask them as why do you want to be what you wish or rich? The answer will be that getting what they wish or becoming rich will make them happy.

If I tell you secrets of life which can make you happy permanently, will this astonish you? I think surely you will want to know the greatest secrets of a happy and blissful life. These secrets were evolved by the ancient Indian Rishis and Yogis. These secrets tap into the universal curiosity about the keys to enduring happiness and well-being.

A Yogi is someone who has found balance in their body, mind, and soul. He lives life according to a Yogic-life style. Have you seen a Yogi? He is simple, mystic, and happy yet living the highest purpose of life spreading his aura wherever he goes and whomsoever he meets.

These Yogis, who were ancient Indian scholars and mystics, delved deeply into questions about life, its purpose, and the nature of truth. They were curious explorers seeking to understand the

essence of human existence. In their quest to seek the what and how of happiness in human-life, these Rishis and Yogis contemplated deep on the questions like what is life, what is the purpose of life, what is truth etc,. Is the purpose of life is only getting 'success' or there is more to it? They sat on the lap of nature surrounded by its bounties away from the din and roar of the busy life. They observed plants and trees; birds and animals; various natural phenomena like sunset and sunrise, flowing and meandering of streams, deep forests and mighty mountains. In this backdrop of natural ambience, their fertile minds germinated with ideas: mundane and spiritual.

In their deep meditation, they unearthed many mysteries about life, the world and the universe. In their relentless quest for discovering the best practices and unleashing the true potential of human beings, they sat for hours, days and years in their deep contemplation and would get up only when they have found the real-truths of human-life. In their deep meditation, they were revealed with the true secrets of life.

Through observing millions of human-minds over years and years, they arrived at the best practices as how to live life happily. These observation and experimentation led them to reveal as what and how to lead a simple, successful, peaceful and purposeful life. For these mystics and Yogis, there are primarily four objectives in life which can make the life of human being a healthy, happy, peaceful and purposeful life. They are Dharama (righteousness), Artha (wealth), Kama (pleasure) and Moksha (salvation).

Their keen observations led them to discover practices and habits that were universally applicable, transcending time, age, and space. Much like the laws of natural science, these were fundamental laws of life, akin to the universality of the Law of Gravitation.

The fruits of the experiences and revelations of these Yogis have come down to us through their disciples, some of which have been put down in writing. Modern science suggests that we are what our habits are. For attaining this internal, universal and permanent success, these ancient scientists enunciated some habits which can lead one to its full capabilities and potential making him fit to win the world by winning his own mind.

This book lists the Yogic-Habits which are distilled from the teaching and observations of these ancient Indian scientists. Presented in a simple way, these Yogic-habits will tell us how to live our daily life following the universal teaching of these Yogis. They are easy, day to day steps which you can follow so as to be your best version and lead a happy, successful and purposeful life.

Let's live these ancient Yogic-secrets.

Acknowledgments

I am deeply grateful to the Almighty for continuously guiding me to bring out my best for the betterment of others. My heartfelt appreciation goes to my late grandfather, Sh. Ram Prakash Mehra, whose values and 'sanskaras' have woven the fabric of my character, enabling me to become the best version of myself. I owe an immense debt of gratitude to my parents, late Sh. Rajesh Mehra and Smt. Parveen, for their unwavering love and affection. A special acknowledgment goes to my wife, Geetanjali, whose guidance and support have helped me. She has taken on additional responsibilities, managing the household and performing many duties traditionally associated with a 'father' role, allowing me the time to focus on my passions. As the saying goes, "Wife is always right," and indeed, I follow the 'right path.'

My appreciation extends to our children, Dhruv and Udhay, who have been the blessings in our lives.

I am fortunate to have had inspiring mentors and influencers who have played crucial roles in shaping my life. I express gratitude to my grandmother, late Smt. Sumitra Devi, late Smt. Urmil Puri, late Dr. Gurnam Singh, Sh. M.K. Sharma, Sh. Santosh Taneja Ji, Sh. Devender Triguna, Tarun Chugh Ji,

Dr. Vishwanath Sood, Dr. Vatsayan, Sanjeev Chopra (IAS), Sh. Ramgopalji, Sh. B.K. Jha IRS, Suraj Ji, Prf. Anil Gupta Sir, Ramseshwar Ji, Gopal Arya Ji, Sh. Savjibhai, and others who have influenced me significantly. Special thanks to Sh. Rajiv Nagpal Ji, and Sh. Arun Anand Ji.

This book would not have been completed without the constant motivation and support of my friends. A special thanks to Rajesh (Dhoni), Sanjeev Kandhari, Rajubhai, Sanjay, Gourav, Sushant, Mohit, Capt. Arya, and Anshul. I am also grateful to Ashu Vij, Pallavi Vij, Drishti-Mishra, and Madam Smriti for their encouragement. Also, Jaibir ji deservers a special thanks for always editing my books.Very special thanks to Rishikul Yoga at Rishikesh. My interest in Yogic Habits has been ignited by Vipin Baloni Sir and Vimal Sharma. Of late, I have been reading Osho who has influenced my thinking too. I may have inadvertently missed a few names, but I carry all of you in my heart on this journey.

Contents

CHAPTER-1

Find Happiness Within You

चित्ते प्रसन्ने भुवनं प्रसन्नं

(*citte prasanne bhuvanaṃ prasanne*)

When you are happy, the Universe is happy
THE VEDIC QUOTE

Have you ever wondered why you close your eyes on seeing a beautiful view of nature like a snow-peaked mountain or a meandering river or a beautiful sunset? You close your eyes as you want to hold on to that happening by making it a part of your mind's memory. All our pursuits of happiness are meant to make our mind happy. It is projection of our inside on to the outside. When you are happy, the whole world is happy.

Happiness is a state of our mind. It begins and ends within your mind. Our natural state of being is bliss. But, in our misconception, you ascribe happiness to things, thought, persons, places or circumstances. Our unending thinking gives rise to desires which in-turn force us to take action to achieve those desires with a feeling that if you get your desires fulfilled, you will be happy. In your life, you give the key to your own happiness to the world outside which in fact belongs to you and you only.

The Yogic-science suggests that all the happiness is within. There is no outside, external or without factor. It is always within. The moment you realise this simple truth, you realise that you and only you are the source of joy, happiness and bliss. Happiness is living in the moment. It is when you are not missing out anything in that moment.

Yogis suggest three states of happiness:

- Sometimes, absence of unhappiness is seen as happiness. Like, you are suffering from a misery and luckily you are free from that misery. You feel a moment of happiness.

- You feel happiness when your desire is fulfilled. You are longing for a girl and she becomes part of your life; you are happy.
- Observe a child while he is playing. He is happy in himself without bothering about the world. It is a state when you are happy within and your state of mind is free from any desire or outer state of things. You are happy as it is. This third class of happiness is what real happiness is. A Yogi is radiating happiness free from any external validations, conditions or circumstances. Drop any external validation and you are happy then and there. You must attain a state of being happy within for you to be in a state of bliss.

CHAPTER-2

Find the Purpose of Your Life

धान्यानामुत्तमं दाक्ष्यं धनानामुत्तमं श्रुतम्।
लाभानां श्रेय आरोग्यं सुखानां तुष्टिरुत्तमा ॥

dhānyānāmuttamaṃ dākṣyaṃ dhanānāmuttamaṃ śrutam
lābhānāṃ śrēya ārōgyaṃ sukhānāṃ tuṣṭiruttamā

Skill is superior to material things knowledge is superior to wealth. Health is superior to profits and contentment is the best form of happiness.

MAHABHARAT VANPARVA

Have you ever asked yourself what the purpose of your life is? We pursue and live for different purposes in life. Some of us seek wealth; some pursue success, while others strive for peace and happiness. . For some, it is being their best version, or finding their true self. There are also those who believe life has no specific purpose, and others who think in life everything is predestined.

Yogic science suggests that life should have a purpose; it shouldn't be random or aimless. Yogis broadly divide life's goals into four areas covering all the aspects of life. These are called **Purusharthas**. They are **Dharma** (righteousness), **Artha** (prosperity), **Kama** (pleasures) and **Moksha** (salvation) in the same sequence.

Dharma is living life of righteousness. It is fulfilling your duties according to your age, status, time and circumstances. We have responsibilities towards our family, friends, society, nation, and humanity.

Artha is the pursuit of wealth which includes physical needs, material-wealth and richness. Material wealth, such as money, property, vehicles, and modern luxuries, is essential to support ourselves and our families and contribute to society.

Kama is any activities that bring pleasure from a simple act of applying perfume to intimate acts of love. It encompasses the pursuit of pleasures, including enjoying tastes, hobbies, and passions. It includes both recreation and procreation. These pleasures are experienced through the senses, such as seeing art, hearing music, smelling fragrances, and savouring tasty foods.

Moksha is the pursuit of the soul. It is a state of supreme bliss where one is happy as he is, free from the bondage of attachment and aversions, likes and dislikes. It transcends all forms of pleasure and pain.

These four aspects are hierarchical in nature. The base of these Purusharthas is dharma which means you cannot attain any of the other purposes without practising the righteousness. If you earn riches, it should not be at the expense of someone else or by exploiting others: be it human or natural resources. In Yogic-life, pleasure for the sake of pleasure is prohibited. The ultimate purpose of life is Moksha where one works for the sake of work and for society and existence without expecting any rewards.

CHAPTER-3

The Yogic Diet

यथा अन्नं तथा मनः ।।

Yatha Annam Tatha Mannam

Our mind is directly related to the quality of our food intake.

We are what we eat. Our diet influences our physical, mental, emotional energy levels. Therefore, Yogis are very particular about their diet. It is considered that food is the building block of the body; as we eat, so we become in mind and body. We have seven layers of the human body, and the outermost and grossest layer of human existence is the food sheath. The underlying principle of the Yogic diet is that we should eat to live and not live to eat. So, food has to be wholesome, complete, and balanced. Yogic science of Ayurveda states that a perfect diet consists of all the six tastes of food. The purpose of food is to increase the longevity of life span and make this body fit for higher purposes.

According to the Yogic-science, there are three types of foods: **Sattvic, Rajasic and Tamasic**. The Sattvic diet is recommended for real Yogis. It promotes a life expectancy of 100 plus years. It is pure, easy to digest and a balanced diet. It increases energy, happiness, calmness, and mental clarity. The foods included in Sattvic diet are fresh fruits and vegetables, sprouted grains, roots, tubers, nuts, cow milk, curd, and honey.

The Rajasic diet is recommended for men of action. This food causes movement, action, excitement and confidence. It includes flavours that are hot, bitter, spicy, dry, and salty. Deep-fried Sattvic foods are also considered Rajasic.

Tama means inertia and the Tamasic diet makes one inert, dull and enhances anger. The life expectancy is low, and it is bad for health. The foods in this diet include non-vegetarian food, processed, artificial and genetically engineered food. It also includes stale, undercooked-and highly fried foods and high fat foods.

Yogis also stay away from caffeine, tobacco, alcohol, and artificial sweeteners which can lead to spikes and swings in moods. To enhance life and to be happy, peaceful and healthy, you should follow Sattvic diet.

CHAPTER-4

Remove Yourself from Likes and Dislikes

सुखदुःखे समे कृत्वा लाभालाभौ जयाजयौ।
ततो युद्धाय युज्यस्व नैवं पापमवाप्स्यसि ॥

Sukhdukhe Samhe Kritwa Labhaalbho Jayajayo.
Tato Yudhaye Yujaswa Nevam Papamvapsaysi.

Make grief and happiness, loss and gain, victory and defeat equal to thy soul and then turn to battle; so thou shalt not incur sin.

If I ask you to define someone's personality, your mind immediately rushes to explain what you like about him or what he likes or dislikes. It is simple human psychology. We tend to view the world in terms of binary opposites: like and dislike, good and bad, right and wrong. Our upbringing often conditions us to think exclusively in these terms.

Individual likes and dislikes can vary widely, even in something as simple as food preferences. For example, you may have a preference for vegetarian food and a dislike for non-vegetarian options. In yogic philosophy, the idea is to acknowledge these preferences but not allow them to excessively influence one's state of mind or overall well-being. By practicing detachment and equanimity, one can maintain inner balance and reduce the impact of likes and dislikes on their overall happiness and peace of mind. These two opposing emotions of liking and disliking are not inclusive but rather exclusive. If you like someone or something, by default it excludes others or other things. Like and dislike give you feelings of attachment and aversion. This may be for a person, a place, a thought or a situation. This leads to pleasure if you attain the desired ones and pain when you do not get the desired ones. It distorts our perceptions, causing us to magnify the positive qualities of what we like and the negative qualities of what we dislike. There is always a conflict within you for avoiding the aversion and attracting the thought or person of your attachment.

Yogic-way says you should free yourself from these two contradictory and opposite energies. Yogic habits suggest you

to minimise your likes and dislikes. You can start by dropping your one smallest like or dislike. For example, many people have opinion of good or bad on almost everything. You can start by releasing your judgments about things and thoughts that don't deeply concern you.

Starting today, select one of your likes and one of your dislikes, and consciously work on letting them go over time. Gradually, you'll realize that this world of opposites is nothing more than your mind and ego at play. The goal isn't to transform your dislikes into likes, as both likes and dislikes are the source of bondage. Instead, free yourself from the whirlpool of these preferences and ride the waves of emotions rather than being crushed by them.

CHAPTER-5

Reduce Your Desires

आशायाः ये दासाः ते दासास्सर्वलोकस्य।
आशा येषां दासी तेषां दासायते लोकः ॥

– कवितामृतकूपः

āśāyāḥ yē dāsāḥ tē dāsāssarvalōkasya
āśā yēṣāṃ dāsī tēṣāṃ dāsāyatē lōkaḥ

Those who are enslaved to desire, are enslaved to the whole world. But for those to whom desire is enslaved, to them, the entire world is enslaved.

What is a desire? It is a strong urge for something. It has an innate belief that getting what we desire will make us happy. Nature has produced us as a desire seeking creature. Desire is what causes us to act and is kept alive by the fantasy of the object. You might have heard the common feeling, 'Oh, how beautiful it is,' "I will be happy when I get that," etc. It is desire at its full play. Desire has its various fangs: choice, preference, desire, liking, longing, wish, etc.

When Yogic-science talks about desires, it does not mean natural desires like immediate desire for food, thirst, survival etc. They are natural. For Yogis, desire is an impulse directed toward an external object. Desire is mind at its play which generates them through its accumulated experiences. For example, a man projects his own idea of beauty onto a particular woman and sees highest beauty even in an ugly woman and gets attracted towards her.

Yogis suggest us to be aware about the source of our desire. If you look deeply, we have only a few desires but our wandering mind makes us think of many things. Desire effectively becomes a contract with oneself to be unhappy till we get that thing. It is the reason of unhappiness as there is a gap between what you desire and what you are at present. It is impossible to fulfill and pursue all our desires. You cannot have all the things for all the times. Neither is it practical nor feasible.

Yogic-science says that we should minimize our desires to be happy. It acknowledges that you cannot end all your desires, but you can limit them to a few yet core desires. The best way is to list out your main desires and eliminate from your mind those desires which you do not need. Desire-prompted action leads us to bondage of the desires. When our actions are free from the compulsion of desire, we gain freedom and can appreciate the beauty of life without becoming overly attached to it

Destroy the desires through discrimination and meditation.

CHAPTER-6

Thinking 'Nothing'

निरपेक्षो निर्विकारो निर्भरः शीतलाशयः ।
अगाधबुद्धिरक्षुब्धो भव चिन्मात्रवासनः ॥

Nirapekṣo nirvikāro nirbharaḥ śītalāśayaḥ
agādhabuddhirakṣubdho bhava cinmātravāsanaḥ

You are unconditioned and changeless, formless and immovable, unfathomable awareness and unperturbable, so hold on to nothing but consciousness.

Our mind is nothing but a storehouse of thoughts. It is a thought producing and collecting machine. We are born with thoughts and identify ourselves with the thoughts. We are into endless gyrations of thoughts from morning to night, from birth to death. Nature has given us two amazing faculties: Memory for survival and imagination for creation. Both of these are just thoughts. However, we miss life because of the play of these two factors. Either, we are living in memory of imagination. These two tools of our personality devour most of our life. Yogic-science says that you are not your thoughts. Though you have collected and stored them, they are not you. Like if you have collected many clothes in your almirah, they are not you.

For this, just take just 10 minutes in a day when you are thinking 'nothing'. Let you sit in a calm place may be in your office and just observe your thoughts. You may have incoming and outgoing of many thoughts, let them come and go. Do not be carried away by them. Sit and relax. Accept every thought which is surfing up. Do not let yourself be attached or swayed by that thought. In the second stage, just try clearing your mind of thoughts and just observe the thoughts. Say bye to every thought which comes to your mind at this time. This will tell you the source of thoughts which may be emerging from your memory-bed or simply a reaction to outside stimuli.

It will lead you to a moment when you are thinking nothing. In that moment just be yourself: thoughtless and desire-less. Come out

of this thoughtful thoughts and swim in the sea of thoughtlessness. Consciously, do not let any thought be entertained. You will find much relaxation and clarity. Make this Yogic habit of 'nothingness' a daily affair.

CHAPTER-7

Yogic-Habits Vs Goals

ध्यायतो विषयान् पुंसः सङ्गस्तेषूपजायते ।
सङ्गात् सञ्जायते कामः कामात् क्रोधोऽभिजायते ॥ ६२ ॥
क्रोधाद्भवति सम्मोहः सम्मोहात्स्मृतिविभ्रमः ।
स्मृतिभ्रंशाद्बुद्धिनाशो बुद्धिनाशात्प्रणश्यति ॥ ६३ ॥

Dhayato Vishanpunsha, Punsha Sangasteupujayete.
Sangat Sanjayate Kamah Kamat Krodho Bhijayate 62.
Krodhadbhavati Sanmoha, Samoha smritivibransha.
Smritibhranshadbuddhinasho buddhinashatpranashyati.

When a man thinks of objects, attachment for them arises; from attachment desire is born; from desire arises anger. From anger comes delusion, from delusion the loss of memory, from the loss of memory, the destruction of intelligence; from the destruction of intelligence he perishes.

Modern culture focuses on success. To be successful, you should work on achievements, targets and goals. The definition of success is how far you are able to hit on the outer and outwardly achievements in terms of goals. So, it limits the purpose of life on 'goals of life'. However, Yogic-science suggests that life is living, experiencing and being. It is not only achieving something but enjoying life as it is. Life is not a destination but a journey which is to be celebrated each moment.

Action emanates from habits which are nothing but condensed thoughts. Habit forms when we repeatedly do any act. Goals are abstract and intangible wishes prompted by modern competitive ethos whereas Yogic-habits are internal, concrete, day to day living realities. That is why, Yogis speak of behaviors, habits and lifestyle changes for a happy and contended life. Instead of goals and aims, Yogic life focuses on habits which are assimilated in our day to day life, many times in the form of rituals. It is more concerned how to live life than why to live life.

Yogic-science is living in the moment instead of attaching yourself with the future. Life is moment-to-moment. If you set goals, you are attaching to a thing or a moment out there in future. For the Yogis, life is experiencing each moment of the day and consequentially life. It is an existential realty. So, it suggests us to

live in the moment which is the present moment. Present moment is the only realty; rest is either imagination or memory.

If you were to ask a true Yogi about the purpose of life, their response would likely be that life has no specific purposes. The act of living life itself is a purpose. Instead of the results of any action, it suggests us to devout to action. Only if the action is good, it will result to good results. We must focus on action which is our divine duty, the results we should leave to the Almighty. You have control over your habits and not on the results or goals. So imbibe habits of life instead of goals of life.

CHAPTER-8

Make Your Bed

धीरे-धीरे रे मन, धीरे सब कुछ होय।
माली सींचे सो घड़ा, रितु आए फल होय।।

dheere dheere re mana, dheere sab kuch hoye
mali seenche so ghara, ritu aaye phal hoye

(slowly slowly o mind, slowly everything happens)
(gardener waters hundred pots, season comes fruit happens)
Gently gently, O my mind Gently all things go. Tho' you water a tree a hundred times Only in spring will fruit grow

Small is beautiful. We often overlook the power of small, everyday habits. Life of Yogis revolves around their daily routine. They are self-established. Yogis suggest self-work as one of the ways to be productive, efficient and vibrant. For this, one such small habit is making the bed when you get up.

The moment you are up from the bed, you are open to the challenges of the world. The start of the day is time to put you in motion. So, make your own bed. This is the first step towards discipline. It helps to organise you. You realise the value of self-work. When you have made your bed, it is your first success of the day. You get a sense of accomplishment with a very small act. Study suggests that a small act of making your bed can trigger you for other successes by giving you the feeling that you have done something worth.

This habit puts in motion a cyclical change for other good habits of the day. If you want to change yourself, start off by making your own bed. It will not only prepare you for the day but for the night routine also as you have an organised bed when you join the bed after a tiring day. It helps in improving your sleep quality since you have a nice, clean and organised bed to sleep. It is also good for your overall wellbeing and self development.

Yogis are all about self-reliance and self-improvement, and they serve as a great example for us to follow. Yogis are self-workers and self-dependent. So, whether you're starting this habit today or continuing on your journey, remember that greatness often begins

with the simplest of actions. Start from today, start making your bed and feel the difference in your daily routine.

CHAPTER-9

Who is the Pilot?

सोऽहम्

-ISHA UPANISHAD

So 'aham

I am that

Human beings live and interact with the world at different levels of awareness. Our human personality consists of body, mind, and heart. When we think or act, our level of consciousness is always different. When we exist at the level of body, we have physical needs like food and sex. Our emotional personality desires emotional attachment, like and dislikes, appreciation, rewards etc,. When we exist at the level of ego, we have strong likes and dislikes and attachment-aversion towards things, thoughts and persons. However, there is another centre which is above these three well popular centres. It is a consciousness or soul centre. When we are piloted by the soul, we are just the observer.

Yogic-science says that we are always to be aware of who is piloting us. Be attentive to the aspect of consciousness at play. Specifically, we should observe who is the pilot at any moment? While our daily conduct and connect with the outside world through sense, we should be alert and aware about our centre of consciousness: thinking, feeling or observing. Higher form is subtler that the lower one. If the ego with its likes and dislikes is piloting you, be ready to face its repercussions in terms of pain and pleasure. The life is nothing but your ego at its play.

Yogi is a person who is connected to all but attached to none. He exists in the world and does his worldly course without being part of it. His desires do not emerge from the ego-centres but from a higher awareness of soul. He does his duty and is immune from the result of the action he undertakes. Yogic science says to drop the ego-personality and live in soul-personality so as you are free

from any bondage. Always be aware as who is the pilot of your consciousness. Live from heart-centre without being prejudiced from the accumulated past. For this, Yogis use a phrase: **'Sakshi Bhav'**(be an observer) Be an observer to the drama of body-mind and intellect. This observer is free from body-mind-intellect matrix. The moment we realise that our pilot is soul, we are free from emotional and ego-led personality. This is the simplest and the most profound way of being happy and blissful.

CHAPTER-10

Acceptance: This Moment is the Best Which Could Happen to You

आनन्दः अस्ति स्वीकृतिः

Anand asti swikriti.

We are happy only in our acceptance

Life, by its very nature, is in flux, ever-changing and unpredictable. It presents us with a continuous flow of experiences, some delightful and others challenging. In our pursuit of happiness and success, we often encounter setbacks, disappointments, and unexpected turns. It's during these times that the attitude of acceptance can be a beacon of light, guiding us through the storm.

We live in either imagination or memory. These two faculties are rare gift of nature for us humans to survive and progress. We rarely live the present. We either crib why it happened to us or wish something good could happen to us. Our life oscillates between 'should' and 'should have', stealing the joy of 'is'. These two are the patterns of Chiita (mind-stuff). We can live beyond the mind only when we understand that memory and imagination are just pattern of mind.

Yogic-science advises us to live as the life exists. Acceptance doesn't mean resignation or giving up on your dreams and goals. Rather, it's about recognizing the limits of our control and releasing the need to fight and struggle in every aspect of our lives. It is accepting that there are forces beyond our influence, such as nature, the actions of others, and unforeseen circumstances. It is like a game where you play your role, and do your best. If you accept the moment and life as it is, you can be always happy and in a state of bliss.

The most significant gift of acceptance is the ability to find peace in the present moment. When we resist what is, we create

internal conflict and suffering. By accepting the current situation, we free ourselves from unnecessary turmoil and open ourselves to the potential for growth and positive change.

You should plan but do not get frustrated if and when your plans go haywire. We are just a small atom in the bigger scheme of the galaxy of universe. The life is a combination of efforts and destiny. You should develop an attitude that this is the best that could have happened to you or is happening to you. Do not expect better or something different. Accept the life as it comes. We struggle when we propel the life as we wish the life to be. The only change we can bring about is changing ourselves. To see the life as it is or as it happens and enjoy it as an observer is the way to simple life.

CHAPTER-11

Who AM I?

'तत् त्वम असि'

'Tat tvam asi'

Meaning: You are that.

You know what is the biggest question in life, as per Yogic-science? Who are we, truly? We question ourselves as who we are? Though we ponder over this core question of life, but with our limited understanding, we are not able to discover who exactly we are.

Consider, for a moment, your desires for wealth, happiness, and success. Who is this 'you'? In introducing yourself to others, you typically mention your name, family background, profession, and social status, all of which are bestowed upon you by 'others'. Even your name is attributed not to you.

Suppose, you have collected many things over the years and stored them in your cupboard, these are your things but can you say the things are you? All your wealth and collections manifested in your various assets like a car, a luxurious bungalow and many other physical things; are your possessions and not you. We confuse our possessions with our self.

Some argue that we are mind and intellect. We have many thoughts, emotions and ideas. In the due course, these thoughts and emotions make your memory, intelligence and personality. You have five senses through which your mind collect ideas from the outside world and your mind sends it to your personality which 'reacts' to these ideas by either liking or disliking depending upon the predisposition of your personality or ego. These ideas are then filtered to the intellect which decides the course of action. This decision of the intellect is transmitted to the mind which gets the things manifested or executed through five organs of action. Mind

is collection of thoughts and ideas which each one has different owing to different experience and its reactions to it. So, we are also not mind. Are we a personality with likes and dislikes, good and bad feelings? What we call 'this is me'? Not, obliviously.

If we are none of the above who we are? The ancient Indian Yogic-science suggests we are what we remain after we have negated all the above covering of body, mind and intellect. The three covers of body-mind-intellect change and are subject to time, space and decay, so they are not 'I'. We are that permanent and ultimate truth which guides and controls all of us and which is living inside all of us. This is the only realty which is changeless and eternal. We are the extension of the larger universal soul. People call it by various names. The nature of this 'I' is Truth-Consciousness and Bliss which is a state of permanent bliss. The only purpose of life is discovering this 'I' by uncovering and undressing the false cover.

CHAPTER-12

Live Beyond Mind

जीवेषु करुणा चापि मैत्री तेषु विधीयताम्

jīveṣu karuṇā cāpi maitrī teṣu vidhīyatām

Meaning: Be compassionate and friendly to all living beings.

Empiricism, rational-thinking and logic are the hallmark of modern thinking. We are trained to think in a logical way from the beginning. You get stimuli and decide your response on the basis of your logical-rational mind. This rational mind is basically a survival-mode mind which gives you the best alternative out of the given options where you can survive the best.

As per Yogic-science, mind is not only rational it is beyond rationality also. Rationality, logic, intellectualism are only one aspect of our mind. They are collectively known as thinking. Mind stuff has five patterns: knowledge, false-knowledge, imagination, sleep and memory. You are beyond the mind-stuff. You can be yogic only when you are aware about these five patterns of mind-stuff and transcend them.

Live beyond senses and beyond the logic. Live intuitively and with your feeling. Feeling is different from thinking. For example, you have a dog. He has a feeling of love for you that cannot be explained by logic of rationality. Feelings like love, passion or compassion cannot be verbalized but they exist. You know you have the feeling but what and why you have the feeling is beyond the realm of intellect.

When you feel, you live in the present. You are not in the thinking-mind. Mind is nothing but an accumulator who keeps absorbing everything. The moment you are free from these accumulation known as memories, you are in the present. You are not thinking but being. Present moment or the feeling is just one moment ahead of the mind.

As a Yogi, you have to be attentive, alert and aware of this present moment and always be ahead of the mind otherwise any present moment identified with mind becomes a memory the very next moment. When you are aware and conscious of the present moment, you are no more a mind. Mind can only exist in either past or in present, nowhere else. Find who is working behind these five patterns of mind and who the witness of these patterns is. That is the true living and being.

CHAPTER-13

Count Your Blessings

अन्तो नास्ति पिपासायाः सन्तोषः परमं सुखम् ।
तस्मात्सन्तोषमेवेह परं पश्यन्ति पण्डिताः ॥

- MAHABHARATA VANAPARVA

antō nāsti pipāsāyāḥ santōṣaḥ paramaṃ sukham
tasmātsantōṣamēvēha paraṃ paśyanti paṇḍitāḥ

There is no limit for greed, and contentment is the ultimate happiness, so a wise man is always happy with what he has.

Yogic-living suggests acknowledging of our beautiful existence. It is based our accepting the life as it comes to us. One of the simplest and easiest ways to live a contented life is to count your blessings. In our compulsive thinking, we tend to question what we do not have and forget what we have. When we compare our life with less fortunate, we get an idea how much blessed we are. We have so many blessings.

We crib that we do not have this or that material things be it a car, a big house or a particular brand of dress. A person was cribbing that he did not have a nice pair of shoes when he saw a person without legs!

Health itself is a great blessing. Yogic-life says you to be aware of your blessings be it material things or thoughts without getting attached to them. Mere living and existing in is a blessing. Ask a dying person, he will tell you the value of life. Nature is full of blessings in terms of fresh-air, mountains, rivers, forests and so on. You have just to pause yourself and devour the bounties of the nature.

A simple Yogic-habit is to make a list of the possessions you have in your life and which you need for your daily life. This simple Yogic exercise make you realise how much blessed you are and how many things you need in your life. Discard any idea, thought or memory also which is not needed by you. Live life need based and not greed based.

Never ignore your blessings, never loose awareness of them.

CHAPTER-14

Beyond Achievements: Embracing Yogic Wisdom for Detached Action and Inner Fulfillment

कर्मण्येवाधिकारस्ते मा फलेषु कदाचन।
मा कर्मफलहेतुर्भुर्मा ते सङ्गोऽस्त्वकर्मणि ॥

Karmanye Vadhikaraste ma phaleshu kadhachana.

Never consider yourself to be the cause of the results of your activities, nor be attached to inaction.

Meaning: You have a right to "Karma" (actions) but never to any Fruits thereof.

In our limited understanding, we tend to follow success in the most selfish way. In our daily living, we are more concerned about the result of an action than the action itself. Mothers are more concerned about the marks of the children than the level of effort they have put in. You are attached more to the profits of your business than running the business itself.

Seeking result or reward of action is not bad. But attaching yourself with the reward of any action makes you bound. Suppose, you want to be the best in your field, but there are other people also who are better than you. Despite your best efforts, you do not achieve that status, you feel frustrated. So, desired result of any act is and can never be in your hands. It is logical also from the worldly point of view. Many people desire to get one thing. Logically also, only one person will get that particular thing, rest will not get it.

Yogic-science suggests that you should de-orient yourself from the reward of any action. You have a duty to act but have no right or control over the result thereof. If you are attached more to the result or reward to your action, you are concerned about future which may not be as desired by you. You are fretting away your energy in the imagination of the reward instead of using that energy at hand for making the action itself better. The best way to be in flow of an action is to absorb yourself in that action wholly, completely and totally.

So our duty is only towards giving our best and leaving the rest. Give up the desire to enjoy the result and reward of your

action to your ideal or God. This is the easiest way to end the internal tension and conflict in you.

CHAPTER-15

Sunrise to Sunset: Embracing Yogic Wisdom for a Purposeful Daily Routine

कराग्रे वसते लक्ष्मीः करमध्ये सरस्वति।
करमूले तु गोविन्दः प्रभाते करदर्शनम्॥

Karagre Vasate Lakshmi, Karamadhye Saraswati
Karmule tu Govindah, Prabhate Kardarshanam

Meaning: At the top of the hand resides Goddess Laxmi and in the middle of the hand resides goddess Saraswati. At the base of the hand resides Lord Govind. We should take a look at them in the morning.

Your life is a sum total of days you live. Yogis speak of **Dinacharya** which means daily routine. Dinacharya is a Sanskrit word made up of 'dina' meaning day and 'acharya' meaning activity. How you spend your day is how you spend your life. A daily routine is absolutely necessary to bring transformation in your body, mind, and consciousness. To live a simple and happy life, you have to make a set routine.

The basic science behind the Yogic-routine is to live as the universal live. It is aligning you with the nature's rhythm. It suggests that we human are the extension of the planet. So, it suggests us to get up when the universe gets up which is the time of sunrise. Getting up before sunrise (Brahmmurta) is relaxing. After getting up, you should do the body cleaning which includes the basic function of elimination and cleaning of your tongue and taking bath.

Your day should be divided in four parts: One for your work, one for health and meditation, one for your passions and the last one for sleep. The day should start with health and exercise which includes healthy and balanced meal. The second aspect is family and leisure. Proficiency and earning wealth is part of the day to sustain life and family. Following these broad categories of areas, you should excel without compromising any of the areas or aspects. The aim of living the life spreading in days is to follow four **Purusharthas**.

The purpose of the day is to give your full in each areas. No area or aspect is either inferior or non-important. Your day should synchronise with the rising and falling of the sun. So you should try to complete your day including your meals by the sunset and in no condition beyond that. Let everyday start with meditation and end with meditation. Remember a good day spend is the basis of a good life.

CHAPTER-16

Nature's Dance: A Yearlong Exploration of Observing and Embracing the Seasons

द्रुमा सपुष्पाः सलिलं सपदम्, स्त्रीय सकामाः पवनः सुगन्धीः।
सुखाः प्रदोषाः दिवसाश्च रम्याः, सर्व प्रिये चारुतरं वसन्ते।।

druma sapushpa: salilan sapadam, stree sakaama: pavan: gandh:.
sukha: pradosha: dayaashch ramya:, sarv priye chaarutaran base.

Oh dear, the trees of spring are full of flowers, the waters full of lotuses, the winds full of their fragrance are blowing pleasantly, making both evening and day pleasant with those scented winds, which make women full of sensuality. And thus everything is exceedingly pleasing now

Have you ever wondered why your mood gets suddenly elevated when it rains outside? The Yogis have answered it. For the Yogic-science, our body is the microcosms of the macrocosm planet. What happens outside in the environment also affects our internal body-mind-intellect matrix. Nature affects us on moment, hourly and daily basis; and also a shift in the seasons in nature affects us profoundly. As there is variation in sunlight, temperature, humidity in each period of the day, there is also variation in lengths of daylight, levels of humidity, and temperature shifts during the changes in the seasons.

Our body requires different types of foods, water-intake and sleep according to seasons. A day in summer has different impact on our energy levels than a day in winter. If our bodies adjust properly by desiring different types of food, altering our sleep/wake cycle according to sunrise and sunset, and changing our energy levels, we maintain homeostasis and all is well. It is to be expected that when autumn sets in, we desire warmer, heavier foods and have a tendency to sleep more. Summertime brings about a longing for cool drinks and light fare, staying up late and rising early with the sunrise.

For this Yogic-science suggests us to align ourselves with the nature on daily basis (Dincharaya) as well as when there is change in seasons (Ritucharya). We have to observe the changing seasons which reflect not only change in environment but suggests that change is a permanent philosophy of the world. We have not only to protect our self from the vagaries of the changing seasons but also flow with the change. Day routine, food, clothing and living should be in tune with the seasons.

Do observe these shifts in seasons for a healthy, long and productive life.

CHAPTER-17

Harmony of Being: Exploring the Inseparable Bond Between Humans and the Planet

यथा पिण्डे तथा ब्रह्माण्डे,
यथा ब्रह्माण्डे तथा पिण्डे।

"Yatha Pinde Tatha Brahmande,
Yatha Brahmande Tatha Pinde"

As with the self, so with the Universe. What is going on within you is same as what is going on in the Universe.

Have you ever wondered that we humans are an extension of the Planet? A human body is made up of **Panch-Tatva,** the five elements: Air, water, earth, space and fire. In the same way the Universe is made up of these five elements. We eat a part of the planet daily as our food. We are, what we eat. This part of the planet that we eat as food becomes a part of our physical body in no time. Our physical body evolves from the planet and finally merges in it. We are born, we live and grow in the lap of mother earth, which nourishes us like a mother takes care of her child in her womb.

According to the ancient Indian knowledge, our existence and well-being is inseparably related to the well-being of the planet. Like the mother's bond with her child, this relationship is intertwined, interdependent and mutually co-existent. It is an inseparable bond.

Nothing can better explain the relationship of the planet with the human being than the oft-quoted Yogic aphorism which says, **"Yatha Pinde Tatha Brahmande, Yatha Brahmande Tatha Pinde"**, which means the outside exists what is exactly inside us and vice versa. It simply means as is the human body so is the planet, as is the planet, so is the human body. As is the individual so is the universe, as is the universe so is the individual. Man is a microcosm or a mini-planet of the macrocosm, that is, the planet. Does not it surprise you that the percentage of water in human body is 71% which is almost same as on the Planet? The same is the case with the ratio of air and earth element.

So, the existence of a human being cannot be thought of without the existence and well-being of the planet. If the outer world (the planet) is healthy, we humans can be healthy. The inner and outer-world are alike.

For a Yogi, outer surroundings are as important as inner body. Until and unless you take care of the outer environment, you cannot take care of the inside.

CHAPTER-18

Organize Your Desk

युक्ताहारविहारस्य युक्तचेष्टस्य कर्मसु।
युक्तस्वप्नावबोधस्य योगो भवति दुःखहा।। 6.17।

– BHAGWAT-GEETA

yuktahara-viharasya yukta-cestasya karmasu
yukta-svapnavabodhasya yogo bhavati duhkha-ha

Meaning: He who is temperate in his habits of eating, sleeping, working and recreation can mitigate all material pains by practicing the yoga system.

Yogic science says that every action you do is not something external but an internal act of your personality. It reflects your inner affairs.

One of the simplest yet highly productive Yogic habits is to organise your desk. If you work in your office or have desk at home, the clutter on the desk reflects how organise or unorganised you are. Yogic science suggests us to live on essentials and organise what we have.

Plenty of unnecessary things take away your focus and energy. As a matter of habit, simplify your desk. Discard what you do not need on day to day basis. Keep the desk in an organised manner where the things should be placed at their respective places.

Also, the golden rule is keeping the things you use more near your dominant hand or in front of you. You can group similar things together. Cleaning up your desk before leaving either in office or in home can save much of your time.

If you organise your desk, you organise your internal thought process and make a habit of being organised. It helps you to withdraw from unnecessary and focus on the core. It makes you and your mind de cluttered. In your daily household routine also, make your bed, clean your room, set your cupboard, set your dress and keep your washroom clean and health. Keeping the household items at their respective place can save you much time, energy and resources. An organized desk can work wonders for your productivity and peace of mind. It's a simple yet effective way to improve your work environment. You feel better at work and at your **Karmbhoomi**.

Soon this habit extends to other areas of life.

CHAPTER-19

The Equanimity of Mind

योगस्थः कुरु कर्माणि सङ्गं त्यक्त्वा धनञ्जय।
सिद्ध्यसिद्ध्योः समो भूत्वा समत्वं योग उच्यते ।। 2.48 ।।

– THE BHAGWAT GEETA

yoga-sthaḥ kuru karmāṇi saṅgaṁ tyaktvā dhanañjaya.
siddhy-asiddhyoḥ samo bhūtvā samatvaṁ yoga uchyate

Meaning: Be steadfast in the performance of your duty, O Arjun, abandoning attachment to success and failure. Such equanimity is called Yog.

The Yogic-science is living inward. It is going to the source of anything and everything. For this, you should know your mind. You have to win your mind to win the world. Your mind consists of thoughts. Any thought has two aspects: rational and emotional. Our mind mostly works at emotional level and we use our rational mind to justify our emotions, openly or secretly. Even the modern studies confirm that we are emotion driven.

You are attached to any situation in proportion to your emotional investment to that situation. The Yogic science aims us to reach a state called ***Sthithpragya*** which is the equanimity of mind. In this state, your mind is completely, absolutely and totally free from its emotional drama and the bipolarity of likes and dislikes, good and bad, expectations and worries.

The Yogi is always in his mind which is in equanimity, a state of balance. Yogic mind is not swayed by the inherent forces of mind but you control the flow of thoughts. It is an observer's mind where all thoughts are seen as flow of river which is ever flowing.

To reach this level of mind, Yogic science suggests to slowly taking each situation dispassionately and without any preconceived notions. Look at the life and situations in life not as it should be but as it is. This will bring equanimity in thought and therefore action. For this, you can start with one action each day which should be free from your own inherent tendencies (**Vasnas**). Decide one action in a day where you will act upon without any emotion led desire and also keep yourself free from the expected result of that action. This will bring slow detachment from action, emotions and consequently from the mind. You will lead a balanced life.

CHAPTER-20

Focus Mastery: The Blueprint for Cultivating a Successful Life

गते शोको न कर्त्तव्यो भविष्यं नैव चिन्तयेत्।
वर्तमानेन कालेन प्रवर्तन्ते विचक्षणाः।।

gate śoko na kartavyo bhaviṣyaṃ naiva cintayet
vartamānena kālena vartayanti vicakṣaṇāḥ

Meaning: We should not fret for what is past, nor should we be anxious about the future; men of discernment deal only with the present moment.

The word Yoga evolved from the Sanskrit word 'Yuj' which means to join. When you join all the forces at your command and focus on one ideal, you are Yogic. The thing of focus may be material or non-material. The process of focus with all your energies is Yoga.

One of the best habits of success is inculcating the habit of being focused. Positive psychologists describe this as a **flow state** which is complete immersion in an activity. As per this flow theory, you can achieve efficiency up to 600 % if you are in flow state of mind.

In Yogic code of habits, Karma is an action when you absorb yourself in the chosen flow of work or thought. You are at your best version when you are immersed in your work. This state is when your body, mind, intellect and soul are at same level and are laserised on your work at hand. Yoga is absorption in action. You should be so absorbed that you should not be concerned about the result or reward of the action. It gives a state when you have no sense of time, space or external world. Start with a thing or thought which you are good at. Now, put your physical, emotional and intellectual world in that. You will realise that you can reach a state of super-productivity and efficiency in no time.

It gives a state of ***Yoga Karma Su Koshlam, Karma Su Koshlam, Yoga*** (perfection in action and action in perfection) in which individual is absorbed in the action-state forgetting and giving up reward for the action. Focus on action and not on the result. Rejoice the action. Let your each action howsoever insignificant it may be a Yogic-action flowing like music from a flute.

CHAPTER-21

Embrace the Art of Living Through Action

कर्मण्यकर्म यः पश्येदकर्मणि च कर्म यः।
स बुद्धिमान्मनुष्येषु स युक्तः कृत्स्नकर्मकृत ।। 18।।

karmaṇyakarma yaḥ paśhyed akarmaṇi cha karma yaḥ
sa buddhimān manuṣhyeṣhu sa yuktaḥ kṛitsna-karma-kṛit

Meaning: Who sees action in inaction and inaction in action, he is the wise man, the yogi, the doer of all actions among men.

Yogis are man of action. Yogic-science says that you cannot remain without action for even a moment. This universe is in action every moment. The sun, the moon, rivers all are in action. Your body, heart, pulse and other organs are in relentless and continuous action even when you are sleeping. Only the dead do not act. So, being in action is an existential realty instead of any compulsion. You follow the universe and act.

Action can be divided in to desired action and non-desired action. Yogic-science suggests us to do desired action which one has to undertake as per his duty depending upon one's state of life and role in life. If you have dexterity in action of the role assigned to you, you are doing good action. For example, if you are a father, your action is to be the best at it. If you are a professional be best in it. Your every act should be a class act which means not only the best from your standards but from the standards of the society.

For Yogis, action is neutral, neither good nor bad. It is the intention which makes an action good or bad. Even the smallest act of brushing your teeth can be a class action if the intention behind this action is good, and an act of helping other can be bad if you are doing with a selfish motive. The test and touchstone of any action is not how far it is successful in the eyes of the world but how much it transforms you.

Inaction is termed as suicide. You are made to act by the nature. You cannot live without action even for a split-second. Your ***Karmbhoomi*** is not the world but your mind. Do your action to polish your inside and not for the outer things. Your personal

victory is precursor to public victory. Only by evolving inside, you can succeed outside.

CHAPTER-22

Posture Mastery: The Key to Confidence, Health, and Presence

तत्रैकाग्रं मनः कृत्वा यतचित्तेन्द्रियक्रियः।
उपविश्यासने युञ्ज्याद्योगमात्मविशुद्धये ।। 12।।
समं कायशिरोग्रीवं धारयन्नचलं स्थिरः।
सम्प्रेक्ष्य नासिकाग्रं स्वं दिशश्चानवलोकयन ।। 13।।

tatraikāgraṁ manaḥ kṛitvā yata-chittendriya-kriyaḥ
upaviśhyāsane yuñjyād yogam ātma-viśhuddhaye
samaṁ kāya-śhiro-grīvaṁ dhārayann achalaṁ sthiraḥ
samprekṣhya nāsikāgraṁ svaṁ diśhaśh chānavalokayan

Meaning: Seated firmly on it, the yogi should strive to purify the mind by focusing it in meditation with one pointed concentration, controlling all thoughts and activities. He must hold the body, neck, and head firmly in a straight line, and gaze at the tip of the nose, without allowing the eyes to wander.

Motion leads to emotion. Many times physiology impacts psychology to a great extent. Posture affects our emotions and thoughts, and vice versa. Modern research also corroborates this fact. For example, slouching makes it easier for negative thoughts to pop up while an upright posture encourages empowering thoughts.

Yogis are aware about the power of posturing. The mystic of yore have experimented and developed various postures for a healthy living. A good posture is both relaxing and stability at the same time (**Sthir Sukh Asana**). The three state of posturing is: sitting, standing and walking. For all these states of being, Yogis have evolved the best posture so as we can be relaxed as well as peaceful and productive. Further, Yogis have also suggested ill-effects of bad posturing. Good posturing can avoid and prevent many ailments in future.

You will find a Yogi always in a different posture while sitting, walking and even sleeping. Body postures include the movement of hands in various positions so as energy flow is proper and in rhythm. Posture plays a very significant role in terms of transmission of energy throughout the body. To revive the **Chakras** (7 body-energy points), we have to align our body to our natural posturing.

Yogis are very particular about their posture. Living a Yogic life is to develop a very good yet comfortable posture in day to day life. It is aligning your body with the rhythm of the Universe. In your day, do observe your posture. It will help you to be more

aware about your body, its movements and surroundings. If there is a bad posture, try to mend it. When you meditate, you must be sitting a meditative posture with your backbone upright and aligned. This posture is called **Samadhi** posture. Good posturing brings alignment in your body, breadth and thought.

CHAPTER-23

Be Authentic You

स्वात्मानं बोध ।

Swatmanam Bodha- Ancient Indian quotes

Meaning: Awaken to your true self

We all are born with uniqueness. We have different biological code, desires and outlook. The purpose of life is to identify your uniqueness. What is unique you? We are swayed away by what others tell us. We are seldom being we. Teachers, friends, knowledge, Gurus are good for information and guidance but what you really are, is only known to you. No one else can tell you.

Yogic-science says discover 'Yourself' and be your authentic version and not someone or somebody else's version. You can be happy only when and what you do is original you. Someone may be good at games, someone may be good at music and some other may be at some other aspect. We move out our mind to seek guidance as to what we really are but ironically fell trap in the opinions of others of what we are without actually realising who we are. That is the biggest trap.

In the era of social-networks, likes and dislikes from others decide your happiness. Getting approval and validation from others is not a proper way to live. It is giving the key to your life to others to decide. It is also giving others the key to your happiness and sadness. If you do not know who you are, how can you expect others to know who you are?

Yogis know who they are and they do not seek validation of their true being from others or the outer world. Their touchstone is their own mind and not the mind of others. Others' opinion is others' opinion. So, discover who you are by working on yourself without others certifying you who you are.

Yogis encourage individuals to reflect on their own desires, talents, and uniqueness, and to live in a way that is true to themselves rather than trying to fit into someone else's mold. This path is more likely to lead to a genuine sense of happiness and fulfillment. Be you and live that authentically. And, all you should do is what you want to do.

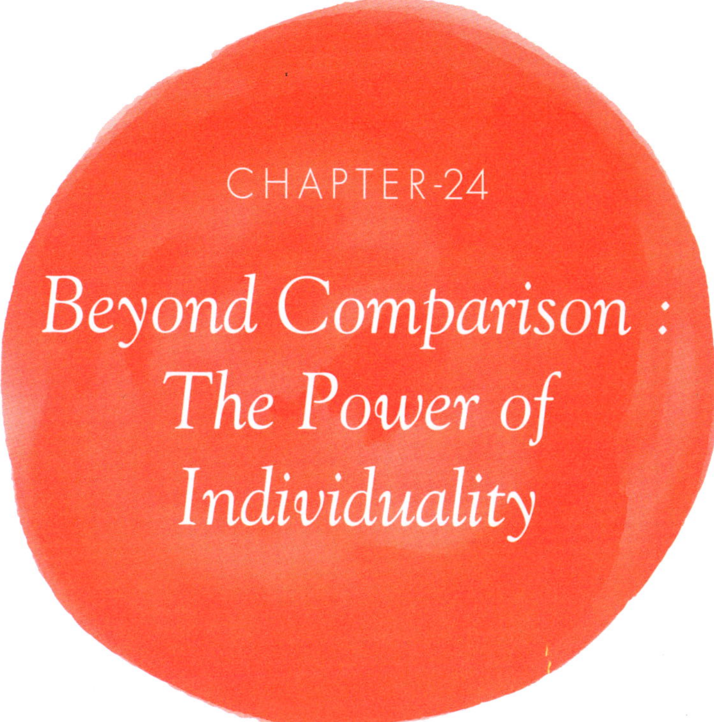

CHAPTER-24

Beyond Comparison : The Power of Individuality

श्रेयान्स्वधर्मो विगुणः परधर्मात्स्वनुष्ठितात्।
स्वभावनियतं कर्म कुर्वन्नाप्नोति किल्बिषम् ।। 47 ।।

śhreyān swa-dharmo viguṇaḥ para-dharmāt sv-anuṣhṭhitāt
svabhāva-niyataṁ karma kurvan nāpnoti kilbiṣham

Meaning:It is better to do one's own *dharma*, even though imperfectly, than to do another's *dharma*, even though perfectly. By doing one's innate duties, a person does not incur sin.

The surest way of being unhappy is comparison. You compare your past with the present, you are unhappy. You compare your unborn future with the present you, you are unhappy. You compare yourself with others, you are unhappy. You compare one situation with another, you are frustrated. We compare when we work from the level of our ego. I have a personality which is superior or inferior from others. When it is assumed as superior, it breeds ego. When it is assumed inferior, it creates ego. It is as simple as this.

Nothing is comparable. Absolutely nothing is. Even your own fingerprints are not the same. As per Yogic-science, every moment, person or situation is unique. No two moments can be alike. No two persons can be alike. It is the simplest realty. Everything is changing, moving, in a flux. Relish this. Comparison takes away your happiness. The only unchanging is the change.

Our mind is so preoccupied with the past and future that we hardly spend a fraction of our time in the present moment. The best way to end comparison is to live in present. Present when free from either the comparison of past or future is a bliss. Present in itself a complete and full entity. Live and observe everything as it exists. Our mind is nothing but a collection of memories. Memories are nothing but moments passed by. The moment you align with your mind, that moment becomes memory. You are just one moment ahead of your mind, the next moment that becomes memory.

You are happy when you are fully absorbed in the present moment. Be aware of the present moment and observe if you are living that moment. Yogis are masters of being present and fully aware of the richness of each moment. They never compare with anyone, anything and anywhere.

CHAPTER-25

Mindful Prioritization: The Key to Purposeful Living

आलसस्य कुतो विद्या, अविद्यस्य कुतो धनम् ।
अधनस्य कुतो मित्रम्, अमित्रस्य कुतः सुखम् ।।
Alasasy kuto vidya, avidasya kuto dhanam
adhanasya kuto mitram, amitrasya kutah sukham

Meaning: Where is knowledge for a lazy person (there in no knowledge meant for a lazy person), Where is wealth for ignorant/ foolish (There is no wealth meant for ignorant); Where are friends for poor person (There are no friends of a poor person) and How one can be happy without friends.

What most people lack in life is a priority. They are not clear about what to do when. Priority is doing right thing at the right time. Yogic-science says that you should live every moment giving due importance to what is due and required in the moment and in life.

A seemingly good action which does not fall in the priority list cannot be termed as a good action. Even if, any action is good but is not in your priority as per moment and state of life, that action is a bad action. A priority less life gives rise to regrets. If you live life without priority, you miss the core of life.

Yogic says the three priorities in life are: self-care, love and purpose. These priorities are in the same sequence. Rest all is intangible, imaginary and secondary. The first priority of life is self care .i.e. health and happiness. You cannot enjoy life without a good health. Your only asset is health which is the physical wellbeing, emotional vitality and good mood. If you cannot self-care, how can you care others? The second in priority list is other's care which is love. After you have done self care, loving and spreading happiness should be a priority. It is your relationship with family, friends and society in general. The third priority is your mission and purpose in life. This is the purpose for which you

have come to the world. It may be your unique passion or a sense of giving back to society through your unique talent.

Nothing else matters in life. Health, love and your mission is what should be your priority and your whole life and days should revolve around these three areas in the same sequence.

CHAPTER-26

Sacred Echoes: Transforming Affirmations through the Power of Mantras

ॐ भूर्भुवः स्वः तत्सवितुर्वरेण्यं
भर्गो देवस्य धीमहि धियो यो नः प्रचोदयात्।

Om Bhur Bhuvaḥ Suvaha Tat-savitur Vareñyaṃ
Bhargo Devasya Dheemahi Dhiyo Yonaḥ Prachodayāt

Om, the Lord, is earth, the space in between and the heavens. That Lord is the one who is the most worshipful. We meditate on that effulgent, all-knowledge Lord. May he set our intellects in the right direction.

Yogic-science posits that the whole universe is nothing but vibration. The universe evolved out of cosmic-sound. Even scientifically, the basic units of creation: electrons, protons and neutrons, are only energies in varying states of vibration. The entire universe is made up of energy, and this energy in different states of vibration makes up the objects of the universe. So it emphasises on chanting Mantras.

Chanting ***Mantras*** is a Yogic-method in which you recite or affirm yourself on a small *Mantra* (thread of knowledge). Mantras are not words or sentences just put together. Besides being words with deep meanings, they are also vibrations. The second most used sense of human body to connect to the outer world is ear which is the carrier of the sound.

Sound and recitation have profound impact on your mind. It focuses your waving mind in to set of ideas or thoughts. This chanting can be done with sound or silent mantras. Yogis have developed many such mantras which are the crux of life in a sentence. It helps you to internalise the idea by repeating it in your mind or by reciting it.

Some mantras have even the alphabetic image like the sacred **OM** mantra. Mantra chanting is connecting back to you with the help of sound and focus. It channelizes all the energies and vibrations of mind towards a single thought. Like modern ways of self-affirmations, mantras have tremendous powers of self-focus, self healing and self-love.

Chanting mantras is said to help develop one's mental powers and strength, ease stress, and take one to a higher level of consciousness. Chanting also improves one's memory and power of concentration, so crucial if one wants to be an achiever.

Yogis recite mantras using the energy of sound to be at peace, productive and bliss. You can also initiate yourself in self journey by invoking these powerful mantras.

CHAPTER-27

Fantasies : Mastering the Mind's Theater

योग चित्त वृत्ति निरोध

"yogas chitta vritti nirodha"

Meaning: Yoga is the stilling or controlling of the modifications or fluctuations of the mind."

As per *Patanjali's Yogasutra*, out of the five patterns (Vrittis) of mind, two are memory and imagination. Our mind is the most amazing projector in whole universe. Its imaginative capacity is unparalleled. It projects a situation which stimulates our desire to achieve that situation. This desire may be for a person, place or a thing. These desires are as natural to our mind as breathing is to our living. Out mind does not make distinction between fantasy and reality. So, it creates a mental-world where we can feel happy. At a given point of time, we are living and spending our 90 percent of time in our fantasies.

These fantasies and imaginations play a significant role in defining the boundaries of our personal growth as human beings. They make us creative, innovative and naïve. Do observe your imaginations. You become what you consistently imagine. If you are thinking and thinking about sensual pleasures, you are surely going to waste your life in these pleasures only. If you are wool-gathering and living in some unreal world you are doomed to fall.

The imagined world is just a fantasy and has nothing to do with the realty. Since, fantasy is one of the Vrittis of mind, it should be used to enhance the reality and not shroud the reality.

Yogic-science says that you should channelize all your imaginations in to the present action in hand. If you are able to make your imagination inward, all your thoughts will merge in you without creating any tension or desire for the outward. You suffer because you imagine and misconceive that imagination as reality. Instead of being a victim of imagination, use this to enhance your life purpose. Yogi has a control over his fantasy and uses that to focussing on reality. Bring back all the powers of your mind to work at hand. The present movement lived totally is the best moment.

CHAPTER-28

The Power of Less

**अशीमहि वयं भिक्षामाशावासो वसीमहि।
शयीमहि महीपृष्ठे कुर्वीमहि किमीश्वरैः॥**

***aśīmahi vayaṃ bhikṣāmāśāvāso vasīmahi
śayīmahi mahīpṛṣṭhe kurvīmahi kimīśvaraiḥ***

Meaning: Let us eat the food we have begged; let the sky be our clothing; let us lie down on the surface of the earth; what have we to do with the rich?

We need a few things to survive and still less to live a happy life. Yogic-science says that there is a power in being less be it wishes or possessions. When you have less, you have to less focus on that. When you have more things and thoughts, you tend to be confused by the clutter of non-essentials.

When you develop a habit of living less, you live with the most important things in life. Yogic-habit is limiting your life to small yet core things of life. It helps you to prioritise the most significant things and avoiding the unessential. We keep accumulating thoughts and things out of sheer habit. Possessions give us a sense of security and comfort.

Make a list of areas, thoughts and things of your life which you consider to be important to your life. It may include spheres like your health, family, profession, leisure, finances and social service. Jot down everything which is not essential in your day to day life and right away start discarding them. For example, you have subscribed to newsletters, emails, social-media notifications. Unsubscribe from these notifications and clutter. Make your desktop free from icons. Free your mobile from not used mobile-apps.

Now, focus on what the core areas of your life is and start following them. Rest all is wastage and share waste of time. You will regret doing more non-essential things than doing a few essential things in life. It will help you focus on quality in life than on quantity. Yogic life is not minimal but optimum living where you can devote most of your time on what is best for you.

You have a limited time and space on this beautiful planet, live optimally.

Bookish Bliss: Nurturing Reading as a Habit

विद्यां ददाति विनयं विनयाद् याति पात्रताम्।
पात्रत्वात् धनमाप्नोति धनात् धर्मं ततः सुखम्॥

Vidya Dadati Vinayam Vinayad Yati Patratam.
Patratvaddhanamapnoti Dhanadharmam Tatah Sukham.

Meaning: Knowledge gives you discipline, discipline comes from worthiness, from worthiness one can get wealth, and from wealth one can do good deeds, and from the combination of all these things can make you to feel pleasant and joyful.

The ancient Indian Yogis used to read and meditate on great ideas and thoughts. For these mystics, reading scriptures was part of their daily routine. Many of these great ideas were handed down through oral traditions. Their observation of best human practices and experiences have crystallised in the form of legendry scriptures like **the Geeta, the Yogasutra, the Ramayana** etc,.

Reading books is one Yogic habit which is simple yet highly effective in self development and growth. You learn the gist of the life long experience of the composer. Habit of reading is one such asset you carry throughout your life. You get ideas, opinions and viewpoints which churns your inside. You learn not only how to achieve the purpose of life but why to achieve it. If self help books give you how to live life, spiritual books give you the very purpose i.e., why of life.

Yogis are great readers. Their sphere of literature spread not only to the realm of spirituality but temporal areas like efficiency, self-improvement and purposeful life. If you do not have a habit of reading, start reading randomly any book or article of your interest, hobbies or passions. When you have developed interest in reading, do start with a list of best books of the world.

Do make notes of books. It is not important how much you read, but it is important to digest whet you read. Take out time from your daily routine and invest an hour for reading. The best possession a Yogi can carry is a library of books. Reading is invaluable. The best way to learn any idea is to practice it. This habit should be inculcated as a family habit.

CHAPTER-30

Reveal the Unseen: Embracing Reality Beyond Identity

अहङ्कारं बलं दर्पं कामं क्रोधं च संश्रिताः ।
मामात्मपरदेहेषु प्रद्विषन्तोऽभ्यसूयकाः ।। 18 ।।

ahankāraṁ balaṁ darpaṁ kāmaṁ krodhaṁ cha sanśhritāḥ
mām ātma-para-deheṣhu pradviṣhanto 'bhyasūyakāḥ

Meaning: Blinded by egotism, strength, arrogance, desire, and anger, the demonic abuse Me, who am present in their own body and in the bodies of others.

We develop our identity during our childhood. It is the result of parenting, schooling and host of situations we encounter. Our identity becomes a reality for us. My identity is how I view myself and the outer world. It is also known as ego. We try to transform every outer thing, situation or person as per our inner identity/self.

Our life is just a play of pleasing our ego and repelling what is not 'fit into' our ego. It is as simple as this. The problem is that we are not even aware about our so called identity-ego. Major part of our identity-ego is formed when we are children and how we respond to a particular situation.

Yogic-science says go beyond your ego-identity. If you want to see the reality, grow out of your limited ego-identity. Your ego is your conditioning. To enjoy the life, you must shed your conditioning and see the life as it exists. Your desires are your ego-led expectations and wishes. Your ego decides what you 'should be' which is the basic reason for creating tension. Contrary to this belief, life is what you are.

Observe the source of any thought. Trace out how you reach to a particular conclusion. Find out whether that idea is the product of objective situation or you arrive at that conclusion because you have been conditioned in that way from your childhood. Observe your each and every habit and trace out their roots. You will find that most of your habitual responses and personality is the product of random incidents and your sporadic response to them.

Yogic habit suggests you to live life beyond the ego-centric desires and wishes and enjoy it. The purpose of life is to be aware of your ego-identity and transcend it so as you can live life as it exists.

CHAPTER-31

Know Your Mind

प्रमाणविपर्ययविकल्पनिद्रास्मृतयः

pramā aviparyayavikalpanidrāsm taya.

Five Vrittis of mind: (These are) right knowledge, indiscrimination, verbal delusion, sleep, and memory.

Yogic-science is a science of mind. The first step of being a Yogi is knowing what mind is? You are what your mind is. Mind if understood is your best friend, and if untamed is your worst enemy. Mind has its moods, patterns and modifications. The Yogis of the lore have discovered the real psychological dissection of mind. So, to be a Yogi, you should know your mind.

Yogic-science suggests that human mind has five patterns: knowledge, wrong knowledge, fancy, sleep and memory. Our mind lives and remains in these five patterns. Mind interacts with the outer world through five senses. Mind captures the world through senses: eyes for seeing, ear for sound, nose for smell, mouth for taste, skin for touch. But senses can capture only those things where mind focuses.

Yogi acknowledges and understands these patterns of mind. Mind lives in time and space. It is there and then. It has only two aspects: words and images. If you stop verbalising your mind in terms of words and images, mind is nothing but silence.

Our mind is the desire-projector machine. When it thinks of what has happened in the past, it is in memory. When it projects expectations, it is in fancy. When we are sleeping, our mind is working without the senses being outward and we absorb in the inner world. Everything we capture through senses fall in either or all these five patterns.

To shed these patterns is living and knowing your real self. To live a life of Yogis, we have first to be aware of these patterns. You

are above and beyond them. Rather to transcend these patterns is discovering you. You are what remain when mind is not at play. After knowing these patterns of mind, the next step is to go beyond them. If you want to follow Yogic-life, you should meditate beyond the modifications of mind and reach at real you.

CHAPTER-32

Blissful Living: Embracing Five Yogic Paths to Happiness

श्रद्धावान्ल्लभते ज्ञानं तत्पर : संयतेन्द्रियः ।
ज्ञानं लब्ध्वा परां शान्तिमचिरेणाधिगच्छति ।।

śhraddhāvān labhate jñānaṁ tat-paraḥ sanyatendriyaḥ
jñānaṁ labdhvā parāṁ śhāntim achireṇādhigachchhati

English translation: ***A person who attains reverence and who has subdued the senses is entitled to receive this knowledge and upon attaining it, he immediately attains spiritual peace.***

One of the purposes of Yogic-life is to be happy which is known in Yogic-science as a state of Bliss. The Yogis aim for a perfect state of mind known as **Sat-Chit-Anand** (Truth, Awareness and Bliss). This is a state of permanent happiness. It is not a destination but a process. This happiness is to be lived in our day to day life. Yogic-way suggests some of the easiest ways to be happy.

The first way of being happy is to absorb you in the present-moment. Whatever you are doing or working at, just absorb yourself in that activity. While doing this you should not miss out any other thought or action. Enjoy the flow of the moment and flow with it.

The second way is to reduce the number of desires at any given point of time. Just focus on only one core desire at a time which should be an important desire for you. Multi desire makes you unfocussed and confuses your mind.

The third way is to still your mind. Mind is not an entity but a process. It is collection of thoughts. It is a very difficult state. However, you can start by realising that thoughts are as natural to mind as waves to the ocean. This state is first step towards a no-mind state.

Reduce your '*should*'. These 'should-be' is the product of your upbringing and socialising. You have opinion, thoughts and preferences for anything and everything. For example, if someone asks your opinion about anything, you express it even though

you may not know the subject of that issue may not concern you. Reduce your opinions to limited things. The word 'should' creates an internal tension since you try to get an external validation.

The last way is to be an observer. For a thought to come, there must be a thing, an object and thinking. Your mind is observing a thing through the thinking. You are neither the thinker, nor the thing or thought. You are neither mind nor patterns of mind, you are just **Sakshi** (witness) to it.

CHAPTER-33

Priorities Your Values

गुरुर्ब्रह्मा गुरुर्विष्णुः गुरुर्देवो महेश्वरः।
गुरुर्साक्षात् परब्रह्म तस्मै श्री गुरवे नमः।।

"Gurur Brahma Gurur Vishnuhu Gururddevo Maheswaraha Gururssakshat Param Brahma Tasmaishree Guraver Namaha"

Meaning: Teacher (Guru) is Brahma (The creator), Vishnu (The Saviour), Shiva (The Destroyer), and also considered to be Param Brahma (The Supreme God). I put "namaskaram" to such Guru.

Man searches for various purposes in life. These purposes emanate from the values he has. Values are like your mental DNA. Everyone has a different value-system and hence different purposes in life. If you want to evolve, you must know which value in life you prioritise more.

As per Yogic-science, there are three prime values: peace, happiness and success. Peace is one prime value which every human aspires. Peace inside and peace outside is the basic condition of any existence. You cannot attain anything without peace. Peace and happiness are intertwined. If you are at peace with your inner and outer world, you are happy.

Happiness is peace in motion or in working. When you are doing something and are happy at doing that, you are at peace. Most people confuse outer success with happiness. For Yogis, success is the outer manifestation of our inner happiness. For Yogis, success is not something outside; it is just the extension of inside happiness.

Every individual has a different priority system of these three values. We as common people live in a delusion that something out there can give us lasting happiness and peace. This is the biggest delusion in the world. Seeking happiness outside or happiness through validation of others is a myth. Since, we are desire-prompted creatures; we think that attaining desires of thoughts, things and persons may make us happy.

For Yogis, the first and foremost value is happiness. This happiness is not coming out of any material success but through being at peace with oneself. For them peace and happiness are the

sides of the same coin. Their success is how far they are internally happy.

A Yogi is happy as he is. His happiness is not desire led. His happiness is here and now. For him, right now and right here is everything. Neither, he postpones his happiness for any future moment. Living in the present moment, enjoying it totally and act with selfless motive is being a Yogi.

CHAPTER-34

Routine Reflection: Observing Your Daily Habits

कल करे सो आज कर, आज करे सो अब।
पल में परलय होयगी, बहुरि करेगा कब॥

Kal kare so aj kar aj kare so ab,
pal mein parlay ho jayegi, bahuri karega kab

- Kabir

Meaning: Do not put off the work for tomorrow which you can do today. When will you do, since life is transitory?

Time has three dimensions: past, present and future. Your life is interplay of these three dimensions of life. We as human spend a very small portion of our time in the present. Yogic science suggests us to live in the present i.e. here and now. Yogis say that present is the only realty.

The two amazing faculties of human mind are memory and imagination. Memory of the past is a must for our survival and existence. Imagination is necessary for our growth and evolution. But the problem comes when we attach emotionally to either of them, and we habitually do.

We compare our present with the past or imagined future. Past gives us a felling of regret. Our mind wishes, anticipates and expects different than our present realty. It creates a desire which makes us unhappy till we achieve that desire. Past is for survival, future is for creation. Bur, present is an existential realty. If you are to create a future, it can only be through and in our present.

The oscillation of the pendulum of past and future takes away the happiness of present. Yogic-science says that living in present is the only truth. You should be aware of this truth and this truthful awareness is a state of bliss.

If you spend more time in past, you are more prone to frustrations in life. Past is nowhere except in your head. Spending time in thinking of future makes you away from the reality and thus creates tensions. Observe as to how you spend your time daily. How much time you live in the present moment and how much time you spend in past and future will help you to realign your life. By observing where you spend your time you can immediately bring back your awareness in the present. You can make a timeline of your life in which you also include your expected years of life. What are the core areas and aspects of life you are spending your time in? You can also do a time-audit at the end of the day in which you count for where and how of the time spent in the whole day.

CHAPTER-35

Skillful Happiness: Nurturing Joy in Everyday Life

आनन्दः अस्ति स्वीकृतिः

Anandah asti svikriti

Meaning: Happiness Is Acceptance

Skill is an art which you learn. For Yogic-science, happiness is not only a state of natural existence but you can learn the skill of being happy. In fact, all the Yogic-techniques are aimed at teaching us the skill of being in bliss. Happiness is not accidental but is an art which can be learnt.

When we live at the level of ego, we are happy when something confirms to our ego-identity. We are unhappy when our ego is not satisfied. The modern ways of dopamine driven happiness are short-lived and temporary. This art of being a state of bliss can be learnt by first unlearning the short term methods of happiness and relearning the Yogic methods.

This art of being happy may be learned either being aware of your true nature or living in action or through meditation. A Yogi develops the habit of being happy by sharpening his skills of happiness. There are various techniques of being in happiness like living in the present, breathing mindfully, being an observer etc.

The best way of learning the skill of happiness is to practice it. The Yogis spend months and years in perfecting the art of being in peace and in meditation. You should develop your own happiness skill index which should be based on these Yogic-practices.

Finding happiness is small things, expecting less and limiting your desires can make you happy. Instead of thinking life as a struggle or competition, for Yogis life is a play. Like a child plays and immerses himself in the play, you have to play the game of life.

For this flowing with the flow of life is the best way. Here you do not create a tension with yourself, but you just live life as it is. Your living is being. Instead of transforming the outer world, Yogic-science suggests to transform yourself.

CHAPTER-36

Yogic Mind

बन्धुरात्मात्मनस्तस्य येनात्मैवात्मना जितः ।
अनात्मनस्तु शत्रुत्वे वर्तेतात्मैव शत्रुवत् ।।6।।

Bandhuratmatmanastasya yenatmaivatmana jitah
anatmanas tu satrutve vartetatmaiva satruvat

Meaning: For him who has conquered the mind, the mind is the best of friends; but for one who has failed to do so, his very mind will be the greatest enemy.

Mind is a thought making machine which has two dimensions of memory and imagination. Our life is interplay of what 'should be' or 'should have been'. Either we want our present to be different or regret why it was not different. Yogis use mind to be beyond mind. First, you have to be aware of the functioning of the mind. It works in the binary of opposites: good-bad, sad-happy, like-dislike. It cannot see the life in totality.

Mind is never in present. It can never remain for a moment in present. If you are in present, it is not mind, it is awareness or consciousness. So, when you are in present, you are aware of the moment and surroundings. You are working from and in your awareness. You are beyond mind. The moment awareness exists, mind wanes.

Awareness is free from any preoccupation or expectations. You are fully absorbed in the moment at hand. Yogis suggest that this is the only reality. This is life. Rest all is either illusion or delusion. You have to live in this awareness and expand it. This is the only truth, this is the only reality and this is the only bliss.

Most people live at the level of mind only. Live your life being alert and aware of the mind and beyond mind. This will give you a dimension much deeper and wider than the mind. When you transcend mind, you are free from the mind. You are not an ordinary person who is bogged down by the mind. Instead, you rule the mind and thus rule the world: inner and outer.

Be aware of the mind and its play. Your whole world is nothing but the projection of your mind. Being aware of your existence and existential reality is being in Yoga or a Yogi.

CHAPTER-37

Breathful Living: Exploring Yogic Respiratory Wisdom

प्राणायामेन युक्तेन सर्वरोगक्षयो भवेत्।
अयुक्ताभ्यासयोगेन सर्वरोगस्य सम्भवः।।

pranayamena yuktena, sarva-roga-kshayo bhavet
a-yuktabhyasa-yogena, sarva-rogasya sambhavah

Meaning: By proper pranayama, all diseases can be cured, by improper practice, all diseases are possible. (hatha-yoga-pradipika)

Breathing is existential as the moment you are born till you die, you do breathing. It is beyond your conscious mind. Yogic-science suggests that it is only through breathing that you are connected with your body and mind. Breathing connects you with the universe. It is the closest thing to you in the Universe. Your mind is nothing but a breath in action. Stop breathing for a moment and your mind also stops!

Yogis give much importance to breathing. They call it Pranaha(vital air). Breath is not only air but a container of the vital-energy. Your mind and consequent thoughts in your mind is reflection of your breathing. You can control your mind through breathing. The first step as per Yogic-science is to be aware of the breathing taking place. There are various techniques of breathing.

- The first technique is to observe the gap between the incoming and outgoing breath. When you breathe in and out, there is a pause when you breathe in or breathe out.
- The second simple way is to take deep breathing which is known as naval-breathing in Yogic-parlance. You breathe in deep from the naval and after touching your deepest centre, the breathe goes out.
- For Yogis, breathing is circular. When you inhale, it is the completion of half circle and breathing out completes the circle of breathing. The third way is to observe the breathing when it completes its half and full circle.
- The fourth way is to observe the fusion of incoming and

outgoing breathing which happens when the inhaled breadth is still inside.

Whenever you are sitting idle, observe your breathing. Even just before sleeping, mind your breathing. See the gap and pause between two breaths. It will help you to sleep deep. Breathing is existence. You can control you mind through breathing. The more you observe your breathing, the closer you are being a Yogi.

CHAPTER-38

Yogic Wisdom: From Knowledge to Practical Living

मय्यावेश्य मनो ये मां नित्ययुक्ता उपासते।
श्रद्धया परयोपेतास्ते मे युक्ततमा मताः ।।2।।

mayy āveśhya mano ye māṁ nitya-yuktā upāsate
śhraddhayā parayopetās te me yuktatamā matāḥ

Meaning: Those who fix their minds on Me and always engage in My devotion with steadfast faith, I consider them to be the best yogis.

Our main faculty of knowing life is mind. We use our senses to capture the world, process it through mind and give it a meaning. For understanding life, we use intellect. We use empirical aspect and rationality of the intellect to give a meaning to life.

For Yogic-science, life is way beyond intellect and mind. It is not knowing life intellectually only but totally. It is not philosophical but existential. Yogic life is not what life is but how to live the life. Being is living. So, Yogic-science has developed Yogic-habits which are the core habits to live the life in a Yogic-way.

It is not enough to know what Yogic life is as a science but it is a practical and daily process which is lived day in and out, moment to moment. Knowledge without action is futile and action without knowledge is baseless. So, it is totality of life which includes knowing the life, living in Yogic action and purpose of life. So, Yogic habits are means to attain the Yogic-purpose of life.

'Why' is important in life but for Yogis, 'how' is more important. Many people know the life intellectually but do not put in practice that knowledge in their life. Living life only in words and not in action is a dichotomy. That is why some say ignorance is bliss. A simple Yogic habit is to not only know life intellectually but to live life in all aspects like feeling, intuitiveness and emotionally.

Yogi-in-action is a Yogi who knows Yogic-science and lives in the worldly affairs without being attached by these affairs. For him,

knowledge (Gyan) is only one aspect of life, the other being action (Karma). When he puts all his heart (Bhakti) in this, he becomes a complete Yogi.

CHAPTER-39

Unlocking the Secrets of Yogic Sleep

यादेवी सर्वभूतेषु निद्रारूपेण संस्थिता।
नमस्तस्यै नमस्तस्यै नमस्तस्यै नमोनमः।।

ya devi sarva bhuteshu nidra rupena samsthita,
Namsteye namestye namonama.

Meaning : I pay obeisance thrice to the Devi, who is present in all living beings in the form of nidra. Keep reciting this shloka.

The three states of human existence are waking state, dream-state and deep-sleep state. According to Yogic science, a day is divided into three core activities: work or profession, hobbies and interests, and sleep. Sleep is seen as a fundamental part of health and vitality. Until and unless you have a good sleep, you cannot be healthy.

There are two states of sleeping: a normal state when you have dreams and the state of deep sleep when you do not recall anything. The state of deep sleep state is hailed in Yogic-science as the best as it recharges your body and mind completely.

Yogic-science is very particular about the timing of going to bed and getting up. Doing Yoga as a physical activity improves mindfulness, increases melatonin levels, and helps reduce sleep disturbance. It induces good sleep. The sleeping cycle should be based on the cycles of the sun and the moon. It is your daily charger. For getting up before the sun rises, you must go to bed early.

Your sleeping pattern has a direct bearing on your health. It is not the quantity of the sleep that matters but the quality that matters. If you get a sound sleep even for a few hours, you can feel a new body and new day.

There is a specific technique in Yoga known as **Yog-Nidra** where you experience the deep sleep state even without actually sleeping physically. This technique is used by the Yogis in their daily life so as to get relaxed and improve their productivity and efficiency. You can use this method to get yourself relaxed and rejuvenated.

CHAPTER-40

Embracing What Is: The Power of Acceptance

अह्मस्मि योधः न कदापि खण्डितः

Asami Yodha, na kadapi khandita.

Meaning: I am a fighter. I will never be broken

As human beings, we seek to change everything. There is nothing wrong in change. Change for better brings development, progress and evolution. But our focus of change is wrong. We always think of changing life, things, persons etc,. We tend to change the world instead of changing our selves. One of the simplest Yogic habits is to accept life as it is.

It is acceptance of realty. If we accept life as it is, many things can change. We are free from the tension of changing. There are some stark realities of life which we do not accept. For example: disease, old age or death. We think that these can happen to others and not us. You can either accept life as it is or resist it. Acceptance is a choice though difficult one. It can transform a momentary happiness to permanent happiness.

Accepting the truths of life is to live utterly, wholly and totally. You do not fight with the life but flow with the life. If you accept the reality of death, you are free from any insecurity in life. We do not accept the opinion of others. Just think that the opinion of other is just their opinion. Accept it and move on.

Accepting is a blessing which keep you away from creating friction with anything and anyone. The Indian Yogis accept everything as it is. We are happier and more peaceful when we accepted what had happened instead of constantly fighting to change things. They flow with the flow taking everything as a grace of God. Only by accepting you can enjoy life without being attached to likes and dislikes.

In your ego, you think yourself to be the centre of this Universe. You have to understand that you are not even a grain of sand in this vast cosmos. So, instead of going against the flow of existence flow with it.

CHAPTER-41

Rediscovering Wonder: Seeing Things Anew

धर्म एव हतो हन्ति धर्मो रक्षति रक्षितः ।
तस्माद्धर्मो न हन्तव्यो मा नो धर्मो हतोऽवधीत् ।।

dharm ev hato hanti dharmo rakshati rakshitah.
tasmaaddharmo na hantavyo ma no dharmo hatovadheet.

Meaning: If you protect dharma, then if needed the same dharma which you earlierly protected will protect you"

We are so much conditioned by our past that we do not enjoy newness and freshness in life. Have you ever looked at your body? You are so conditioned to see your past that you do not find anything new in your body. As per the Yogic-science, everything is moving, changing, in a flux. Nothing is static.

You do not see a thing as it is, you see it from your habitual way of seeing things. It becomes so boring that, you do not actually see it. You can not feel it. One of the Yogic-habits given in Tantra is to look at anything as if you are seeing it for the first time. This is one of the methods to bring your attentiveness in the present.

The biggest trouble in modern life is monotony. You get bored after experiencing a thing for one or two times. It will help you to see everything afresh. This will bring newness in your life. You will not see something from the past-perspective but you will add your emotions to the thing. It will help you to live in the present and ward off the habitual patterns of memory-mind.

Imagine the level of change in your relationships when you are free from looking them from your old patterns. You feel your wife a new person, your children new beings, a blessing. The Yogis live life looking each moment as a new and fresh. Every moment is new, creative, fresh and rewarding.

This is the simplest way of living.

CHAPTER-42

Celebrating Accomplishments: Embracing Your Success

हतो वा प्राप्स्यसि स्वर्गं जित्वा वा भोक्ष्यसे महीम्।
तस्मादुत्तिष्ठ कौन्तेय युद्धाय कृतनिश्चयः ।। 2.37 ।।

hato vā prāpsyasi svargaṁ jitvā vā bhokṣyase mahīm,
tasmāduttiṣṭha kaunteya yuddhāya kṛtaniścayaḥ.

Meaning: Slain thou shall win Heaven, victorious thou shall enjoy the earth; therefore arise, O son of Kunti, resolved upon battle.

One of the simplest yet powerful Yogic-habits is habit of acknowledging our achievements. Whenever we resolve to improve upon ourselves, a thought flashes across – Have we wasted, our precious time and life? It is but natural to think so, when we feel that as per the world's standards, we have fallen short of expectations. This is factually not true as we are all unique individuals.

Every person has done and achieved something or the other in some field or the other. It may be in the areas of personal-growth, family, business, finances, health or fitness. We must appreciate our past achievements and keep reminding ourselves of the good things that have taken place in our lives. It can really change your mindset from having no achievement in life to a life which is full of actions and wonderful achievements!

Draw a list of all the positive actions you have taken in your life however small they may seem to be. However small these achievements may be like leading a healthy life, choosing a profession of your choice, helping a needy, leading a contented life, sharing something with your friends, starting a new venture etc,. You will find that you have done many things in a positive and progressive way in your life. This will make you more internally rich and productive.

After having made a list of your achievements, let us celebrate even the smallest of the small achievements. Accept even your failures as an experience and not as failures. The golden rule is to remember that it is your life and your achievements and if you do not feel good about your actions then who will?

CHAPTER-43

Existence in Action: Embracing the Essence of Living

बुद्धं शरणं गच्छामि।
धर्मं शरणं गच्छामि।
संघं शरणं गच्छामि।

Buddham saranam gacchami…
Dhamam saranam gacchami…
Sangham saranam gacchami…

Meaning: I take refuge in the Buddha. I take refuge in Dhaman. I take refuge in Sangham.

Yogic-science is a practical life. It is not a philosophy, a doctrine, an ideology. It is a practical way of life. Most people in life are so confused with the 'why' of life that they forget the 'how' of life. We look at the life from a limited perspective. We look life intellectually and not totality.

For Yogis, being is living. Life is living every moment, every second, every tissue, and each cell of your body. Life exists, it is the only reality. The simplest way of living is to observe and to live with awareness. Life is not a question to be answered but a mystery to be unfolded, lived and experienced. Your simple existence is bliss.

When you live life as it 'should be', you lose the charm of the present. You must be aware of your existence. Life is not living in some ideal future but here and now. Life is not 'there' and 'then'. Yogis flow with the flow of life. They indulge and enjoy every moment and colour of life. Living life fully is living as being.

It is to take life as it is. Observe the miracles of the universe: rising sun and sunset, changing the weather and seasons, flowing rivers and streams, waves and oceans. You will be in awe of the miracles happening every moment. It is leading life as if it is a play. We are here to play our different roles without being attached to these roles. You are a son, a husband, a father as so on. These roles are to be played in the best possible ways. The more we experience these roles dispassionately, the more we enjoy the life. You have just to be aware of them.

Accept your being and live.

CHAPTER-44

Embracing the Journey: Beyond Constant Goal-Seeking

अनात्मवन्तो हृदियैर्विदष्टा विनाशमर्चन्ति न यान्ति शर्म।
क्रुद्धौग्रसर्पप्रतिमेषु तेषु कामेषु कस्यात्मवतो रतिः स्यात्।।

anātmavaṃto hṛdi yairvidaṣṭā vināśamarcaṃti na yāṃti śarma
kruddhaugrasarpapratimeṣu teṣu kāmeṣu kasyātmavato ratiḥ syāt

Meaning:Those men of no self-control who are bitten by them in their hearts, fall into ruin and attain not bliss, — what man of self-control could find satisfaction in these pleasures, which are like an angry, cruel

We humans are so much goal-oriented that we forget the beauty of journey itself. Our every task is aimed at result, purpose and some achievement. We spend more time in imagining the goal than working on the goal. Life is not just a goal seeking struggle. There are many areas of life where you can work without any end in mind.

For Yogis, life is not something to achieve, attain or reach. Life is not some destination but it is a journey. It is a play. There is a concept of *Leela* in Indian culture where the God creates the world out of His play. So life is play of various things.

This play is like children playing a game. Do they have any goal while playing? They play just for the sake of playing and enjoying. Though they are completely immersed and absorbed in the game, they are not serious about it and enjoy the game for the sake of game. If you ask a child why he is playing, he will reply that he is enjoying the play that's why he is playing.

For Yogis life is a play without being attached to it. It is play without thinking of the result, ends and attainments. Start with small steps. In your daily life, set out some actions which are small, minor and insignificant. Detach yourself from the result of these actions. Slowly, spread this non goal orientation attitude in other areas and aspects of life. This will make you learn to act without a result in mind. You will start enjoying the sheer joy of action. It will bring yogic-attitude in all the acts of daily course of life.

• Live like a Yogi.

CHAPTER-45

Heart-Centric Living: Prioritizing Feeling Over Thinking

अयं आत्मा ब्रह्म

Ayam Atma Brahma

Meaning: "This Self (Atman) is Brahman" (Mandukya Upanishad 1.2 of the Atharva Veda)

As per one study, we humans are 99% 'feelings' and only 1% 'thinking'. But we do exactly the reverse. We only think and do not feel. Surprisingly, most people do not know the difference between thinking and feeling. For Yogis, these are two different, separate and atomic aspects of your mind.

Feeling is a matter of heart while thinking is head and brain. For thinking, you need words to verbalize while for feeling, there is no need to give words. You cannot express your feelings in words. Feeling is conclusion at the first instance. For example, you like a sunset but you cannot tell in words why you like it. For thinking, you come to conclusion only after you have analysed, thought-over and applied your memory. Feeling is universal: even trees, animals and birds have it. However, thinking is confined to humans only.

We are evolved from animals who are mostly instinct and feeling-beings. Animals love unconditionally. Feeling is our natural attribute and not the thinking. However, the instinct of survival has made us thinking and logical beings. Due to this, our feeling faculty has become suppressed. We need to revive it. Many times our thinking is just a cover to our feeling.

Yogic-science says you should feel more and think less. We interact with other living beings through feeling only. If you have a pet at your home, you do not need to express through language with your pet. Both he and you can 'feel' each other.

Thinking is intellect which is only one aspect of the mind. If you live only through thinking, you are living life in segregation

and not completely. Feelings are subtler than intellect. Love and compassion are two natural feelings while hate and aversion are there negative counterparts. They are natural but intellect you have gained through parents, books, religions and others. Yogis live more in feeling than in thinking.

CHAPTER-46

Beyond Thinking: A Path to No-Thought

शनैः शनैरुपरमेद् बुद्धया धृतिगृहीतया।
आत्मसंस्थं मनः कृत्वा न किञ्चिदपि चिन्तयेत्।।

Shane shaneruped budhya drithgrihti. Aatamsanstham mana kritva na kinchidapi chintayan.

Meaning: Little by little let him attain to attitude by the intellect held firmly; having made the mind establish itself in the Self, let him not think of anything.

As per Yogic-science, your mind is nothing but your thoughts. It is collection of all your experiences and impressions saved as memory which is nothing but thoughts. You think through your mind. Thoughts flow in mind like waves, ending and giving rise to new thoughts.

Thinking has different levels and stages. The first level is random thinking. In this, you think randomly and sporadically. Your mind receives a stimulant and it starts weaving a thought process. For example, you see a river, you start thinking of that river, your childhood memories of that river, how that river is different than the other river so and so forth. This wave does not end here only but gives rise to another wave of thought. Our thoughts come as a chain of association with the previous ones. You spend 80% of your thinking in random thinking out of your sheer habit of thinking.

The second level of thinking is contemplation. Here, you select a few thoughts and direct your mind to these thoughts. You exclude many of your thoughts. The thoughts which come are not coming out of chain of association but are limited, filtered and conscious thoughts. The number of thoughts is less compared to the random thoughts.

The third level of thinking is concentration. In this type of thinking, you focus your thought on a particular thing or a person. All other thoughts vanish. You try to limit yourself to know everything about something. The number of thought is far less than the contemplation.

The last level of thinking is meditation. In it there are no thoughts. If there are thoughts, thinking belongs to the first three types and not meditation.

Observe where you exist in this ladder of thinking. Yogis follow the path from random thoughts to contemplation, to concentration and finally end up in meditation.

CHAPTER-47

Harmony Within: Balancing Your Mood

अयं आत्मा ब्रह्म

Ayam Atma Brahma

"This Self (Atman) is Brahman"

(Mandukya Upanishad)

Human mind is moody. Mood changes moment to moment, day to day and also over times. This is the result of waves of emotions in you. The two basic emotions of mood are anger-love and sadness-happiness. These emotions are basically energies of life. If it is positive, we call it love and if it is against we call it anger.

Yogis live a life of mood-neutrality. Whenever we draw out mood, say anger or love, Yogic-science suggests us to locate and go to the source of this mood. If you say you love someone, you draw-out your energy and project it on someone. Similarly, when you feel anger, you project your negative energy on someone.

If you suppress your emotions, you keep your negative energy within. If you express, you vent out your energy on someone. As suggested by the Yogis, instead of expressing or suppressing your energies, just go to find the origin and centre of this energy. Observe. The centre of any of these energies is always within you.

Yogis are able to involve their emotions within its source. Like the waves evolve from the sea and merges in the sea, the emotions evolves and involves within them. If you are able to tap the origin of these energies, you have a potential of living a complete life- a life where you do not give the key to your happiness to anyone else.

When the source of energy is within you, it is foolish to blame or credit others of anything which basically is inside you. If you cannot control your own energies or yourself, how you expect

others to do it for you. The outer things exist in the world but they cannot be the source of your sadness of happiness unless you misbelieve your own self. Following this Yogic-habit, you live totally and holistically.

CHAPTER-48

Daily Thankfulness: A Gratitude Practice

त्वमेव माता च पिता त्वमेव त्वमेव बन्धुश्च सखा त्वमेव।
त्वमेव विद्या द्रविणं त्वमेव त्वमेव सर्वं मम देव देव।।

Tvam-Eva Maataa Ca Pitaa Tvam-Eva
Tvam-Eva Bandhush-Ca Sakhaa Tvam-Eva
Tvam-Eva Viidyaa Dravinnam Tvam-Eva
Tvam-Eva Sarvam Mama Deva Deva

Meaning: You truly are my mother, you truly are my father. You, truly are my relatives , you truly are my friends. You truly are my knowledge, you truly are my wealth. You truly are my All, My Gods of gods.

We take life for granted. We have many things in life be it our material things like a nice home, a good car or intangible things like good health, schooling, family, a good hobby etc,. Gratitude is the habit of being thankful for all the abundance and prosperity we have in life and celebrating it. Gratitude is being thankful, sometimes, for absence of pain or sorrow also! Once a person was unhappy with the pair of shoes he was wearing and was cribbing. Suddenly, he saw a poor little child who had no legs! He was stunned and realized how much he has.

This is one of the best Yogic-practices. For this one of the simplest way is to say 5 specific affirmations in the morning before you get out of the bed. These affirmations be like- I am thankful to God as I am awake and alive, I am healthy and fit, I am having loving siblings and relatives, I am having a good family etc,. Try affirmations for even the smallest things in life like getting a gift, a new friend, a good holiday etc,. Just compare your life with others who are less fortunate in material possession and compare with those who are ahead of you in terms of growth and success.

The first person we have to thank is the Almighty God for the wonderful life that he has blessed us with - . You can also be thankful for the wealth and opulence that he has blessed you and your family with, be it a nice house, a car or friends that you have in your life.

This small Yogic habit can change your entire outlook of life in days and will make you at peace with yourself. You will start finding positive in everything, nay, a positive even in a negative thing.

CHAPTER-49

Simplify Your Life: The Art of Decluttering

क्षणशः कणशश्चैव विद्यामर्थं च साधयेत् ।
क्षणे नष्टे कुतो विद्या कणे नष्टे कुतो धनम् ॥

kshanashah kanashashchaiv vidyaamarthan ch saadhayet.
kshane nashte kuto vidya kan nasht kuto dhanam.

English Translation:- ***One should take knowledge without losing a single moment and save every particle and collect money. The one who lost the moment does not get knowledge And those who consider particle as small do not get money.***

We are privileged with plenty be it books, be it dresses, be it things for daily uses, be it gadgets so and so forth. One of the simplest yet highly effective yogic habits is the habit of de-cluttering. Simply speaking, it is removing unnecessary stuff from your surroundings and living with necessary stuff. Decluttering is simply getting rid of those things which are not required in terms of their cost of space, time and finances. You have so many things around you. Imagine if you remove 1 thing per day, you will de-clutter 365 waste things in a year from your life.

Yogis live with what they require and not in a possessive spree. It is minimum life. Have you observe any animal hoarding anything? When you purposefully de-clutter something from your daily lives, you will realize how much stuff you have and start to evaluate future purchases more carefully and will buy the things you actually require and use, which will ultimately save you money as well. It will help you less to clean, less to organize, less stressful. It will withdraw you from 'non-essentials' and focuses on the 'essentials'.

For this make a list of all the stuff which you use and divide them in 3 categories. Usable items: which you are using currently like your daily stuff. Non-usable items which are waste items and not using like old stationary-items, books, expired items etc,. Non-required items in near future i.e; an item which may not be used in the next 6 months e.g; spare toothbrush, spare stationary, spare diaries, extra staplers etc;. Collect all the non-usable waste items/things and throw them straightway in dustbin. For the stuff which you not require in near future say in 6 months category, collect all such items in a bag and put this polythene in storeroom.

Clean your bed, desk and home. You will find this to be one of the simplest yet highly effective productive Yogic-habits.

CHAPTER-50

Gifting a Belonging Each Daily

अल्पमपि क्षितौ क्षिप्तं वटबीजं प्रवर्धते।
जलयोगात् यथा दानात् पुण्यवृक्षोऽपि वर्धते॥

alpamapi kshitau kshiptan vatabeejan pravardhate.
jalayogaat yatha daanaat punyavrkshopi vardhate.

Meaning: The way a small seed of Bayan tree flourishes with water, the same way the tree of donation flourishes.

It is better to give than to receive, says the ancient Indian proverb. As per a new research, gifting others puts a bigger smile on your face than buying things for yourself. Gifting is one of the most effective habits of personal-development. It is a very simple yet highly rewarding habit which gives an all together different approach to life and the way you possess their material-stuff or belongings, things, items or articles. It is simply giving up one belonging and gifting that belonging to others or some needy!

Yogic science says the purpose of life is to give back to the universe. Life is not just receiving and accumulating. This will make you internally happy and blissful. You are less attached to the material-things and this habit hits at the habit of mindless possessiveness.

For this habit, before you go to sleep, take-out your one belonging which may be a thing, article or item and put it in a collection bag. This bag is like a 'bag of kindness'. The belonging may be anything from a very small article like pen, comb, shirt, t-shirt, clothing, unused-diary, book, pair of shoes etc, to a not so small article like an extra bi-cycle. After a week or so, choose a day and persons to whom these belongings can be gifted. Many people do this act of gifting on a special-day like birth-day or before any festival or New-year. You have to keep in mind that you have to select only one belonging (item) per day and resist from selecting more than one item so that it can form in to a habit.

We are privileged with plenty. We may have many things which are either extras or which we will not require. Let these things be used as gifts to the needy in a positive way.

CHAPTER-51

Daily Mastery: Planning for Success

रात गँवाई सोय के, दिवस गँवाया खाय ।
हीरा जन्म अमोल सा, कोड़ी बदले जाय ।।

raat ganvaee soy ke, din ganvaaya khaay.
heera janm amol sa, kodee pratikriya jaay.

Meaning: Lost the night sleeping, wasted the day eating.

Life is worth diamond, is wasted as priceless.

It is said- How you start your day is how you are going to live your day. And how you live your day is the way you live your life. The quality of your life depends upon the quality of your days! As per one research, 1 minute of planning of the day saves 10 minutes of executing. One of the simplest yet highly rewarding Yogic-habits to be imbibed by in us is the habit of planning his day. It simply means that it is he who is 'running' the day, instead of day running him! You will get maximum out of his day by following this simple habit. It is scheduling and prioritizing your tasks for the day in such a way that it gives you maximum productivity and efficiency. It is giving priorities to your time as well as areas of life.

It is a very simple to follow habit. This simple habit makes you follow your tasks of the days automatically without the pain of remembering them. It helps you prioritize your day and consequently your life and keeps you focused on the areas/tasks which require his focus.

Create a daily routine by making a checklist of tasks before bedtime or right after waking up. Assign specific time slots and durations for each task, and prioritize them from 1 to 10. Be specific in describing your tasks; avoid vague statements. For instance, instead of saying "I will exercise today," specify when and how long you will exercise, such as "I will exercise for 10 minutes after brushing my teeth at 8:30 a.m." After consistently following this routine for 30 days or more, identify your most productive and low-energy times of the day. Check off completed tasks to feel a sense of accomplishment and positive feedback. Ensure your task planning covers various aspects of life, such as health, school, sports, entertainment, and hobbies.

CHAPTER-52

Unleashing Hidden Potentials: The Yogic Habit of Learning New Skills

सुखार्थिनः कुतो विद्या विद्यार्थिनः कुतः सुखम् ।
सुखार्थी वा त्यजेत्विद्यां विद्यार्थी व त्यजेत् सुखम् ।।

sukhaarthinah kuto vidya vidyaarthinah kutah sukham.
sukhaarthee va tyajetvidyaan vidyaarthee va tyajet sukham.

Meaning: ***f you aspire for comforts, leave the knowledge. If you aspire for knowledge, leave the comforts. Aspirant for comforts cannot get knowledge and aspirant for knowledge cannot get comforts.***

As humans, we have multiple opportunities to learn new things and discover the hidden talents and potentials within ourselves. Very often we are either too lazy or procrastinate things and let opportunity pass us by. An attitude and desire to equip oneself with new skills is a must to grow in life. This will help us to discover their real potentials. Every human is born with multiple talents. The good part of learning lies in understanding the potential of a human and unleashing them by encouraging and giving them exposure in the area that interests them. For Yogis, life is to explore and draw-out best in you.

Your talent can be varied: singing, dancing, skating, sports, skiing, creative-writing, telling-jokes or public speaking. So, you have to harness your inborn talent and work on it. This Yogic habit entails learning other than the things what you know in your routine. It makes you bring out your hidden potential of creativity and talent. By learning and being exposed to a variety of skills, you are able to discover your true calling. It makes you happy and satisfied that you are learning to do something that you are passionate about. It helps you to overcome boredom and monotony in life. Life becomes more interesting. It changes the brain chemistry and makes your brain more agile and help in avoiding many diseases like dementia.

For this, list out all the tastes/inclinations you are is excited about. There is no limit to human mind. The purpose of learning new skill is not to be professional in that area. It is learning just for fun sake. Expose yourself to different ideas, games, tastes and skills right from the beginning. Learn at least one new hobby every three months. In a sound personality lives a sound human being.